THE
HINDU
ART
OF
LOVE

delhi — india

EDWARD WINDSOR

THE HINDU ART OF LOVE

·

Fredonia Books
Amsterdam, The Netherlands

The Hindu Art of Love

by
Edward Winsor

ISBN: 1-4101-0000-6

Reprinted from the 1932 edition

Fredonia Books
Amsterdam, The Netherlands
http://www.fredoniabooks.com

Preface

PREFACE

There are three great fundamentals of Hindu civilization: the caste system, child marriage, and the Ars Amoris Indica. The first two have been dealt with again and again in exhaustive fashion.

But a comprehensive work on the Hindu Art of Love which would include the doctrines of the most important eroticists, has never before been attempted in English. The *Kama Sutra* of Vatsya Yana and the *Ananga Ranga* of Kalyana Malla are the only erotics, out of the hundred odd treatises, which have appeared in English translations up to this time.

The ambiguous attitude towards sex in English-speaking countries accounts for this strange omission. And when we consider the fact that in India sexual love has been sanctified to a greater degree than anywhere else in the world, the omission becomes even more deplorable. Nowhere else has the physiological sexual make-up of women been studied with such minute and adoring reverence as in these Hindu erotic treatises.

Apart from its interrelation to the caste system and child marriage, the social and religious significance of Hindu love is such that no one can begin to understand India without some knowledge of it. As the most intimate details of sexual life are discussed in these classic manuals, I have handled the

Preface

subject in the most serious manner. Nevertheless, I have consented to its publication only if privately printed and sold to adults.

EDWARD WINDSOR

Delhi, 1931

CONTENTS

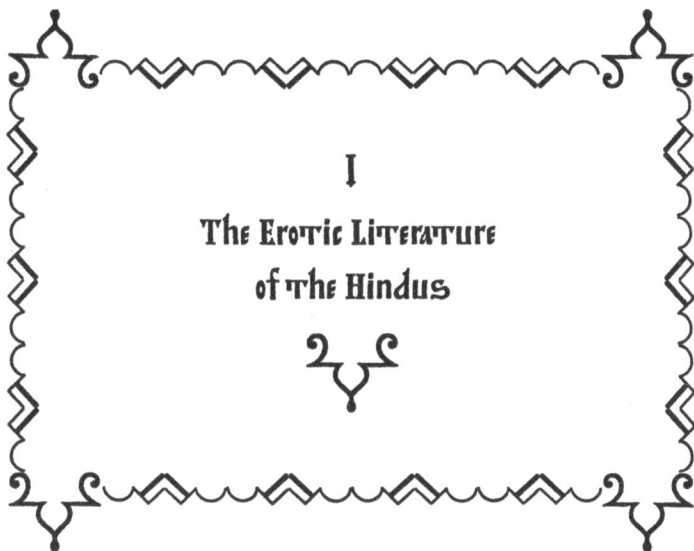

I

The Erotic Literature
of the Hindus

THE
EROTIC
LITERATURE
OF
THE
HINDUS

Love—next to hunger—has at all ages been the strongest motive for the actions of men. As long as the memory of man runs, philosophers have worn themselves out seeking to explain its essence; savants and sages have tried to solve its problems;

poets of all lands and times have never wearied of attempting to find new variations of the old theme of love.

In general, love assumes such great significance that it surprises us but little to find that it reaches overwhelming proportions under certain conditions. Yet in comparison with us, the emphasis upon the *systematizing of sexual love* in certain countries seems fabulous and even grotesque. Such is the case in India, that land of contradictions, where the soul vacillates between sublimity and vulgarity, grace and monstrosity, beauty and deformity, and from the most self-denying asceticism to the most voluptuous debauchery. The blazing fire of the Indian sun, the bizarre splendor of its vegetation, the enchanting poetry of its moonlight, fragrant with sweet-smelling lotus-flowers, and finally—but not the least important!—the characteristic role which the Indian people have traditionally played, the role of the dreamer far away from mortal worlds, philosophic, impractical visionaries: all these unite in making the Hindu a true virtuoso in the art of love.

So in India, love, both its theory and practice, has taken on an all-embracing significance that is difficult for the western mind to conceive. As a preliminary orientation we should like to mention the

The Erotic Literature of the Hindus

following characteristics: The Hindu fanatic sche-
matist divides everything that pertains to mankind
into three great groups:

DHARMA, *the acquisition of religious merit*
ARTHA, *the acquisition of wealth and property*
KAMA, *love, pleasure and sensual gratification*

The crown of the whole *trivarga*, the foundation
of virtue (Dharma) and wealth (Artha), is pleasure
(Kama), the most worth-while pursuit of man.
Hence Lamairesse, the French translator of the
Kama Sutra and *Prem Sagar*, rightly gave them the
title of Hindu Theology, strange as it may appear
at first glance. For they may be considered as pious
works of a venerable, sacrosanct theology: indeed,
erotica plays the same role in India as that of religion in our civilization; it is even more powerful
than the latter and permeates the whole life,
thoughts and emotions of that people.

If we bear this in mind and picture the matchless
joy of the Hindus for systematization, registration
and classification it should not astonish us that they
possess a whole library of erotic works, the like of
which the world has never seen elsewhere and which
makes Ovid's famous *Art of Love* seem like the work
of a primitive.

We wish to caution the reader at the outset not to confuse the term *erotics*, which denote serious works on love, with pornography. We have deliberately omitted all pornographic and obscene aspects of Hindu love as irrelevant to our purpose in this volume.

In order to present to the public for the first time a complete and authoritative work on the Art of Hindu Love we have utilized and included in this work over one hundred Sanscrit treatises and fragmentary sources too numerous to mention, on all the branches of love, seduction and congress. In order not to weary the reader with the immense parade of the names of Hindu eroticists, we here describe only the most important treatises on erotics.

At the pinnacle of erotic literature in India stands the *Kama Sutra* of Vatsya Yana. It is there considered the standard work in the field of eroticism and is held in almost sacred repute. It contains an exhaustive delineation of material in relatively small space; it is a very convenient vademecum, albeit revolting in content, yet an exceptionally welcome supplement to our previous one-sided knowledge of Hindu love. It depicts the Hindu from the cradle to the grave in all the stages of love: as the languishing worshipper of his beloved, as a husband, as an unfaithful adulterer; how he loves, rejoices and marries; how he plays the part of the dandy; how he is occasionally untrue and enjoys the delights of love with the *ganikas* (glorified prostitutes) and other men's wives. All this is described in fascinating detail. We observe life in the harem, the incessant intrigues among the favorites and their companions; we obtain glimpses of the abyss of sexual perversions; we read of recipes for the concoction of all sorts of drugs for all sorts of purposes; in short, the *Kama Sutra* is a veritable thesaurus of information for every Hindu in every department of love.

The fact that the *Kama Sutra* of Vatsya Yana is the recognized authority on the subject in India is not the sole ground for its significance. Its complete importance can only be appreciated when it is realized that this book is not an original treatise but a systematic compilation of the ancient masters in the art of love. Therein lies its principal value. Vatsya Yana drew on the extraordinarily rich experiences of the past and thus was able to present us with a comprehensive view of sexual life in India from time immemorial.

It is impossible to fix the exact date of either the life of Vatsya Yana or of his work. It is generally accepted by modern scholars that he must have lived between the first and sixth centuries of the Christian era.

Vatsya Yana has been reproached for having treated his material in a dry and humorless fashion. Opinions on the stylistic perfection of the *Kama Sutra* vary: if one is dissatisfied with *de gustibus non est disputandum* perhaps the words of Burton may suffice:

"As a collection of facts, told in plain and simple language, it must be remembered that in those early days there was apparently no idea of embellishing the work, either with a literary style, a flow of language, or a quantity of superfluous padding. The author tells the world what he knows in a very concise language, without any attempt to produce an interesting story. From his facts how many novels could be written! Indeed, much of the matter contained in the *Kama Sutra* has formed the basis of many of the stories and the tales of the past centuries.

"It is a work that should be studied by all, both old and young; the former will find in it real truths, gathered by experience, and already tested by themselves, while the latter will derive the great advantage of learning things, which some perhaps may otherwise never learn at all or which they may only learn when it is too late to profit by the learning.

"It can also be fairly commended to the student of social science and of humanity, and above all to the student of those early ideas, which have gradually filtered down through the sands of time, and which seem to prove that human nature of today is much the same as human nature of the long ago.

"It has been said of Balzac (the great, if not the greatest of French novelists) that he seemed to have inherited a natural and intuitive perception of the feelings of men and women, and has described them with an analysis worthy of a man of science. The author of the *Kama Sutra* must also have had a considerable knowledge of the humanities. Many of his remarks are so full of simplicity and truth, that they have stood the test of time, and stand out still as clear and true as when they were first written, some eighteen hundred years ago.

"And now, one word about the author of the work, the good old sage, Vatsya Yana. It is much to be regretted that nothing can be discovered about his life, his belongings, and his surroundings. At the end of Part VII he states that he wrote the work while leading the life of a religious student (probably at Benares) and while wholly engaged in the contemplation of the Deity. He must have arrived at a mature age at that time, for throughout he gives us the benefit of his experience, and of his opinions, and these bear the stamp of age rather than of youth; indeed, the work could hardly have been written by a young man.

"In a beautiful verse of the *Vedas* of the Christians it has been said of the peaceful dead, that they rest from their labors, and that their works do follow them, and remain as a lasting treasure. And though there may be

9

disputes and discussions about the immortality of the body or the soul, nobody can deny the immortality of genius, which ever remains as a bright and guiding star to the struggling humanities of succeeding ages. This work then, which has stood the test of centuries, has placed Vatsya Yana among the immortals, and on this, and on him, no better elegy or eulogy can be written than the following lines:

> " 'So long as lips shall kiss, and eyes shall see,
> So long lives This, and This gives life to Thee.' "

Better to orient the reader at once, we present a topical outline of the rich contents of the *Kama Sutra* with the explanation that the subjects set down will be discussed at some length in the following pages.

I. INDEX AND GENERAL NOTICE OF THE SUBJECT
1. *Salutation to* Dharma, Artha *and* Kama
2. *Observations on the three worldly attainments of Virtue, Wealth and Love*
3. *On the study of the Sixty-four Arts*
4. *On the Daily Life and Amusements of a Citizen*
5. *About classes of Women fit and unfit for Congress with the Citizen*

II. OF SEXUAL UNION
1. *Kinds of Union, according to Dimensions, Force of Desire, and Time; and on the different kinds of Love*

The Hindu Art of Love

The Erotic Literature of the Hindus

Of almost equal importance with the *Kama Sutra* is Kalyana Malla's *Ananga Ranga: The Stage of Love*, sometimes also called the *Kamaledhiplava: A Boat in the Ocean of Love*. Inasmuch as we shall later discuss this work in some detail, we content ourselves at this point merely with a summation of the contents.

CONTENTS OF THE *Ananga Ranga*

I. Of the four Orders of Women: personal peculiarities of the four classes; the nervous, the sanguine, the bilious and the lymphatic woman; the days of the greatest enjoyment of congress for the four classes; the hours which they like best.

II. Of the various Seats of Passion in Women: charts depicting every part of the body and the proper manipulations and caresses for the attainment of the highest pleasure.

III. Of the different Kinds of Men and Women: the men, nervous, bilious and sanguine; also according to length of *lingam:* six, nine and twelve finger-breadths; women, as before; also according to depth and length of *yoni:* six, nine, twelve finger-breadths.

IV. Description of the general Qualities, Characteristics and Temperaments of Women: the qualities attached to the several ages; fifteen causes for the unhappiness of women; signs of indifference of women; twelve periods when women have the greatest desire for congress and at the same time are most easily satisfied; detailed description of the different kinds of *yonis*.

V. Characteristics of Women of various Lands: Description of local Beauties and their charms.

VI. On useful Medicines, Salves, Prescriptions, Recipes, Remedies, Cosmetics, Charms, Magic, Unguents and Spells: for strengthening and restoring potency; for hastening the paroxysm of woman; for delaying the climax of the man; for the enlargement of the *lingam*; for the contraction of the *yoni*; for removal of the body-hair; for ensuring pregnancy; for protection from miscarriage and other accidents; for the ensurance of easy labor and deliverance; for thickening and beautifyng the hair; for enlarging, raising and hardening the breasts of women; for removing perspiration; for causing the mouth to exhale a pleasant odor; for the resuscitation of lost virginities.

VII. The Art of Fascination by the Use of Charms: how to make man or woman obedient and submissive to the charms of the fascinator.

VIII. Of different Signs in Men and Women: how to recognize the signs of vice and virtue in men and women; how to recognize when a woman is enamoured; when she ardently desires congress.

IX. Treating of external Enjoyments: preliminary processes to congress; eight modes of embracing; ten kinds of kisses; seven ways of biting.

X. Treating of Internal Enjoyment: description of the thirty-two main forms of congress; the five great divisions of congress.

The *Panca Sayaka: The Five Arrows of Love* is by one Jyotirishvara Kavishekara. He is called the chief ornament of the poets, the treasure of the sixty-four arts, and the best teacher of the rules of seduction. This work contains nearly six hundred verses and is divided into five chapters, called *sayakas* or arrows. The content of the *Panca Sayaka* follows:

Arrow I. The introduction; the four kinds of women; the lover.

Arrow II. Division of men into *shasha* and women into *mrigi;* all the resulting possibilities of congress; marks of *shasha* and *mrigi;* women of different countries; description of the *yoni;* different kinds of desire; decline of desire.

Arrow III. Removal of bad odor; fragrant oil; perfumes for the bath; general perfumes; means of making the breath sweet-smelling.

Arrow IV. Stimulants; contraction of the *yoni;* winning of the beloved; magic verses; removal of dislike; the raising of hanging breasts; beautification of the *yoni;* removal of body-hair; ease of conception and of the love-fruit; easy labor; description of amulets.

Arrow V. The three organs in the *yoni;* the different kinds of congress.

The *Ratirahasya: The Secrets of Love* is by a poet named Kukkoka, sometimes referred to as Koka. In India the *Ratirahasya* is very popular and has been translated into all the folk-dialects. Burton tells the following ingenious story of the origin of this work: "A woman who was burning with love and could find none to satisfy her inordinate desires, threw off her clothes and swore she would wander the world naked till she met with her match. In this state she entered the levee-hall of the Rajah upon whom Koka Pandit was attending; and, when asked if she were not ashamed of herself, looked insolently at the crowd of courtiers around her and scornfully declared that there was not a man in the room. The King and his company were sore abashed; but the Sage, joining his hands, applied with due humility for royal permission to tame the shrew. He then led her home and performed so persuasively that, well-nigh fainting from fatigue and repeated excitations, she cried for quarter. Thereupon the virile Pandit inserted gold pins into her arms and legs; and, leading her before his Rajah, made her confess her defeat and solemnly veil herself in his presence. The Rajah was, as might be expected, anxious to learn how the victory had been won, and commanded Koka Pandit to tell his tale, and to add much useful knowledge on the subject of congress. In popular pictures the Sage appears sitting before and lecturing the Rajah who, duly throned and shaded by the *chatri* or royal canopy, with his harem fanning him and forming tail, lends an attentive ear to the words of wisdom."

CONTENTS OF THE *Ratirahasya*

I. Introduction; divisions of women into four classes; the days favorable for congress with the different women.

II. A love-calendar: directions for every day of the month for a year so that a man may be able to thoroughly satisfy the desires of the different types of women.

III. Classification of men and women according to length of genitals; the resulting possibilities and combinations of congress; division of the act of congress.

IV. Division of women; reasons for the depravity of women; causes for aversion; the repugnant woman.

V. Treatment of women during congress; the different kinds of love; customs of women in different countries; the twelve kinds of embraces.

VI. Kisses; scratching; qualities of nails; reception and treatment of the beloved; description of the *yoni*; kinds of congress.

VII. How to win the confidence of a girl.

VIII. Marriage; the duties of a wife.

IX. Strange women; stages of love; women to be avoided; cases where adultery is permitted; reasons for reserve; men favored by women; women easy to win; the approach; externals.

X. Winning of women by magic phrases, spells and recipes; how to attain the height of excitement in women;

stimulants; retention of semen; means of enlargement of *lingam*; dilation and contraction of the *yoni*; rules for the removal of hair; for the removal of the fœtus; for easy birth; section on bad odors and pains in the *yoni*; miscellaneous recipes.

Finally, among the most important Hindu works on erotics is the *Smara Dipika: The Lights of Love.* A short summary of the contents of this celebrated classic includes: Description of men; description of women; description of the *lingam* and the *yoni*; the stages of love; sixteen principal kinds of congress; customs in different lands; examination of a girl selected for wife; the four phases of life for women; necessary conditions preceding congress from the woman's viewpoint; the easily won women; how one should protect women; the eight kinds of women as lovers; magic chants and phrases; aphrodisiacs; restoration of virginity; and contraction of the *yoni*.

These five classics are, as we have already mentioned, the most trustworthy and authoritative treatises on erotics and throw more light on the subject than any others. We have therefore given them an extended treatment which we shall not devote to dozens of other works of lesser light. The latter will be mentioned here and there throughout the text whenever any part of their contents proves pertinent; not otherwise, for in a compendium of this nature there is ever-present the danger of being lost in Hindu systematization.

To sum up, then, we purpose in the following pages to present a fairly complete panorama of the sexual life, love and lore of Hindu civilization. We purpose to do so mainly by explanatory extracts and summations from all these works on erotics. Hence, the subject matter is to be regarded as that of the Hindu view. We have frequently made many brief disapprobatory comments but these will be readily recognized as our own. Nevertheless, we have tried not to obtrude our Occidental bias unnecessarily in the presentation of the Process and Practice of the Art and Science of Love and Sexual Congress in India, but have left the eroticists speak for themselves and they are amply able to do so. The reader can thus reassure himself that here, for the first time, is presented an authoritative and historic record of the Hindu Art of Love.

II

The Male Lover

II

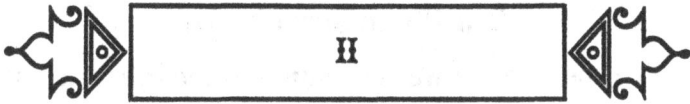

THE
MALE
LOVER

Before outlining the Hindu attitude towards sensual love and its diversified ramifications, we shall consider the role of the *nayaka*, the term referring to a man fit to be a lover of women. There are miscellaneous social requirements for such men which

23

will appear to our western minds as too intricate and too detailed for guidance. But the Hindu thrives upon such mathematical niceties and accepts them slavishly as from some higher command.

The prime requisite is a knowledge and mastery of the *Kama Sutra*. Unfortunately, it is not quite manifest how the rules of the *Doctrines of Pleasure* can be assimilated by the *nayaka* as there are no practical examples and illustrations. It would seem that the dozens of rules and positions in Vatsya Yana and other classic eroticists were incomprehensible unless accompanied by detailed diagrams. Be that as it may, these teachers one and all declare that the study of the *Kama Sutra* is indispensable for a knowledge of love and the Hindu who is not well-versed in its doctrines can never hope to become an accomplished lover or *nayaka*.

In addition to this study of the *Kama Sutra*, though to a lesser degree, the Hindu must acquire a mastery of the sixty-four social arts as set forth in the *Dharma* and *Artha*. These are as follows:

1. *Singing.*
2. *Playing on musical instruments.*
3. *Dancing.*
4. *Union of dancing, singing, and playing instrumental music.*

5. *Writing and drawing.*
6. *Tattooing.*
7. *Arraying and adorning an idol with rice and flowers.*
8. *Spreading and arranging beds or couches of flowers, or flowers upon the ground.*
9. *Coloring the teeth, garments, hair, nails and bodies by staining, dyeing, coloring and painting.*
10. *Fixing stained glass into a floor.*
11. *The art of making beds, and spreading carpets and cushions for reclining.*
12. *Playing on musical glasses filled with water.*
13. *Storing and accumulating water in aqueducts, cisterns and reservoirs.*
14. *Picture making, trimming and decorating.*
15. *Stringing of rosaries, necklaces, garlands and wreaths.*
16. *Binding of turbans and chaplets, and making crests and top-knots of flowers.*
17. *Scenic representations and stage playing.*
18. *Art of making ear ornaments.*
19. *Art of preparing perfumes and odors.*
20. *Proper disposition of jewels and decorations, and adornment in dress.*
21. *Magic and sorcery.*
22. *Quickness of hand and manual skill.*
23. *Culinary art.*
24. *Preparing lemonades, sherbets, acidulated drinks, and spirituous extracts with proper flavor and color.*
25. *Tailor's work and sewing.*

26. Making parrots, flowers, tufts, tassels, bunches, bosses, knobs, etc., out of yarn or thread.
27. Solution of riddles, ambiguous speeches, verbal puzzles, and enigmatical questions.
28. A game, which consisted in repeating verses.
29. The art of mimicry or imitation.
30. Reading, chanting and intoning.
31. Study of sentences difficult to pronounce.
32. Practice with sword, single stick, quarter staff, and bow and arrow.
33. Drawing inferences, reasoning and implications.
34. Carpentry.
35. Architecture.
36. Knowledge of gold and silver, jewels and gems.
37. Chemistry and mineralogy.
38. Coloring jewels, gems and beads.
39. Knowledge of mines and quarries.
40. Gardening.
41. Art of cock-fighting and ram-fighting.
42. Art of teaching parrots and starlings to speak.
43. Art of applying perfumed ointments to the body, and of dressing the hair with unguents.
44. Art of understanding words written in ciphers and the inscribing of words in a peculiar way.
45. Art of speaking by changing the forms of the words.
46. Knowledge of languages and of the vernacular dialects.
47. Art of making flower carriages.

48. *Art of framing mystical diagrams, of addressing spells and charms, and binding armlets.*
49. *Mental exercises in rearrangement of verses, sentences, words, etc.*
50. *Composing poems.*
51. *Knowledge of dictionaries and vocabularies.*
52. *Knowledge of ways of changing and disguising the appearance of persons.*
53. *Knowledge of the art of changing the appearance of things.*
54. *Various games of gambling.*
55. *Art of obtaining possession of the property of others.*
56. *Skill in youthful sports.*
57. *Knowledge of the rules of society.*
58. *Knowledge of the art of war.*
59. *Knowledge of gymnastics.*
60. *Art of knowing the character of a man from his features.*
61. *Knowledge of scanning verses.*
62. *Arithmetical recreations.*
63. *Making artificial flowers.*
64. *Carving figures and images in clay.*

These sixty-four arts are essential propadeutics before a man can become a social success. But the Hindu is well repaid for the study of these arts, if he is to believe Vatsya Yana: "A man who is versed in these arts, who is loquacious and acquainted with the arts of gallantry, gains very soon the hearts of women, even though he is only acquainted with them for a short time."

Even the mastery of these sixty-four social arts does not bring a victorious career to the man. He must in addition possess personal characteristics that are minutely described by the eroticists, dramatists and rhetoricians.

Victorious lovers must in addition be possessed of the following qualities: high birth, learning, knowledge of the world, social tact, knowledge of poetry, story telling ability, eloquence, physical energy, skill in various arts, prophetic vision, deep minds, perseverance, firm devotion, freedom from anger, liberality, parental affection, liking for social gatherings, skill in completing verses begun by others, dexterity in various sports, good health, perfection of physique, virile strength, moderacy in drink, power in sexual enjoyment, sociability, gallantry towards women and attracting their hearts to himself but not entirely devoted to them, independence of livelihood, freedom from envy, and last of all, freedom from suspicion.

Nevertheless, of even greater importance than any of these virtues is a knowledge of the sixty-four social arts. For a man who has mastered them can enjoy women of the first quality. Even if he speaks well on many other subjects but is ignorant of these arts, very little respect is paid to him in the assembly of the learned. On the other hand, a man devoid of other knowledge, but well acquainted with these arts, becomes a leader in any society of men and women. What man will not respect his knowledge, considering that it is respected by the learned, by the cunning and by the *ganikas* (glorified prostitutes). A man skilled in the sixty-four arts is looked upon with love by his own wife, by the wives of others, and by all *ganikas*.

The oldest and most important work of the rhetorical and dramaturgical handbooks of love, the *Bharatiyanatya Shastra*, describes fourteen types of *nayakas:*

"Lover, beloved, sweetheart, master, ruler, life, and joy are the names for the various good properties; villain, sadist, liar, stubborn, braggart, profligate, and savage (uneducated) are the names given the *nayaka* in anger." Then follows a rigid explanation of each of the terms, their sharp distinction from one another and the proper occasions when they may be employed.

The accepted types are usually not so minutely divided and classified. Among other writers only four kinds of *nayakas* are usually named: the faithful, the gallant, the liar, the savage. Some thirty-five works agree in the following descriptions of this quartet:

Anukula: He is faithful who has but one lover and is ever true to her and knows not another.

Dakshina: He may seem to be of two kinds, but is essentially one type. He is gallant who is unchanged in his demeanor to his wife, although his heart belongs to another; he is gallant who treats his beloved ones with equal fashion and equal passion.

Shatha: He is false who speaks and acts friendly in one's presence but speaks and acts unfriendly behind one's back.

Dhrishta: He is a savage if he is unconcerned when he has erred; unashamed at being beaten; mendacious when discovered in the act; publicly engaging in the embrace and heedless of preparing the beloved for the embrace.

We wish to call the attention of the reader to this curious test for it conforms to the sensibilities and moral standards of Hindu civilization though so contrary to our own morality. For morality like customs is often a question of geography and must therefore be viewed sympathetically, especially when it conflicts, as in this instance, with our own sense of decency. In the course of this volume the reader may find other similar differences of morality which should also be viewed with judicious sympathy. This naturally refers only to such modes of conduct as are accepted by the generality of Hindus and practised throughout India.

But to the authentic eroticists all these *minutiæ* are relatively insignificant. To them the root of the entire affair is the size of the *lingam*. This is the real attraction of the *nayaka*. Not whether he is true or false, fat and forty, and so forth, but how many fingers long does he measure? The breadth of a finger is equivalent to half an inch.

Kalyana Malla gives this typical erotic classification in the *Ananga Ranga*:

"There are three kinds of men, namely, the *Shasha*, or Hare-man; the Vrishabha, or Bull-man, and the Ashwa, or Horse-man. These may be described by explanation of their nature and by enumeration of their accidents.

"The *Shasha* is known by a *lingam* which in tumescence does not exceed six finger-breadths. His figure is short and spare, but well proportioned. He has small hands, knees, feet, loins, and thighs, the latter being lighter than the rest of the skin. His features are clear and well-proportioned; his face is round, his teeth are short and fine, his hair is silky, and his eyes are large and well-opened. He is of a quiet disposition; he does good for virtue's sake; he looks forward to making a name; he is humble in demeanor; his appetite for food is small, and he is moderate in carnal desires. Finally, there is nothing offensive in his *kama-salila* (seminal seed).

"The Vrishabha is known by a *lingam* of nine fingers. His body is robust and tough like that of a tortoise, his chest is fleshy, his belly hard, and the frogs of the upper arms are turned towards the front. His forehead is high, his eyes large and long, with pink corners, and the palms of his hands are red. His disposition is cruel and violent, restless and irascible, and his *kama-salila* is ever ready.

"The Ashwa is known by a lingam of twelve fingers. He is tall and large-framed, but not fleshy, and his delight is in big and robust women, never in those of delicate form. His body is hard as iron, his chest is broad, full and muscular; his body below the hips is long, and the same is the case with his mouth and teeth, his neck and ears; whilst his hands and fingers are remarkably so. His knees are somewhat crooked, and this distortion may also be observed in the nails of his toes. His hair is long, coarse and thick. His look is fixed and hard, without changing form, and his voice is deep like that of a bull. He is reckless in spirit, passionate and covetous, gluttonous, volatile, lazy and full of sleep. He walks slowly, placing one foot in front of the other. He cares little for the venereal rite, except when the spasm approaches. His *kama-salila* is copious, salty, and goat-like."

The Male Lover

The *Kama Sutra* deals with the mode of life of the *nayaka* in much greater detail than any other erotic classic. References to the lives of gallants are numerous in Hindu literature but they are usually of fragmentary nature and shed no light upon the subject. Before entering upon this manner of living, a *nayaka* had to undergo a rigid regime of study. We read in the *Laws of Manu*:

"A student who has studied in due order the three Vedas, or two, or even one only, without breaking the rules of studentship, shall enter the order of householders." One of these rules of studentship may claim the attention of the curious: "It is the nature of women to seduce men in this world; for that reason the wise are never unguarded in the company of females. For women are able to lead astray in this world not only a fool, but even a learned man, and to make him a slave of desire and anger."

Having thus acquired learning, a man, with the wealth that he may have gained by gift, conquest, purchase, deposit or inheritance from his ancestors, should become a householder, and pass the life of a gallant. He should take a house in a city, or large village, or in the vicinity of good men, or in a place which is the resort of many persons. This abode should be situated near some water, and divided into different compartments for different purposes. It should be surrounded by a garden, and also contain two rooms, an outer and an inner one. The inner room should be occupied by the females, while the outer room, balmy with rich perfumes, should contain a soft bed of pleasing appearance and covered with a clean white cloth, low in the middle part, having garlands and bunches of flowers upon it, and a canopy above it, and two pillows, one at the top, another at the bottom. There should be also a sort of couch near the head of which rests a stool. Upon this stool should be placed the fragrant ointments for the night, as well as flowers, pots containing collyrium and other fragrant substances, waters used for perfuming the mouth, and the bark of the common citron tree. Near the couch, on the ground, there should be a pot for spitting, a box containing ornaments, and also a lute hanging from a peg made of the tooth of an elephant, a board for drawing, a pot containing perfume, some books, and some garlands of the yellow amaranth flowers. Not far from the couch, and on the ground, there should be a round seat, a toy cart, and a board for playing with dice; outside the outer room there should be cages of birds, and a separate place for spinning, carving and such like diversions. In the garden there should be a whirling swing and a common swing, as also a bower of creepers covered with flowers, in which a raised plot of earth should be made for sitting.

Now the gallant, having got up in the morning and obeyed the calls of nature, should wash his teeth, apply a limited quantity of ointments and perfumes to his body, put some ornaments on his person and collyrium on his eyelids and below his eyes, color his lips with alackta, and look at himself in the glass. Having then eaten betel leaves, with other things that give fragrance to the mouth, he should perform his usual business. He should bathe daily, anoint his body with oil every other day, apply lathering sub-stance to his body every three days, shave his head and face every four days, and the other parts of his body every five or ten days, when the hair is taken out with pincers. All these things should be done with-out fail, and the sweat of the armpits should also be removed. Meals should be taken in the forenoon, in the afternoon, and again at night, according to Charayana. After breakfast, parrots and other birds should be taught to speak, and the fighting of cocks, quails and rams should follow. A limited time should be devoted to diversions with Pithamardas, Vitas, and Vidushkas (traditional characters in the Hindu drama, signifying itinerant jack of all trades, parasitical pimp, and clown). Then comes the midday sleep. After this the gallant, having put on his clothes and ornaments, should converse with his friends during the afternoon. In the evening there should be singing, and after that the gallant, along with his friends, should await in his room the arrival of the woman that may be attached to him, or he may send a female messenger for her, or go to her himself. After her arrival at his house, he and his friends should welcome her and entertain her with a loving and agreeable conversation. Thus end the duties of the day.

We come now to the final classification, that of the friends of the *nayaka*. First, the choice of friends:

> *One who has been a childhood playmate.*
> *One who is bound by an obligation.*
> *One who is of the same temperament.*
> *One who is a fellow student.*
> *One who is acquainted with your secrets and faults.*
> *One who is a child of your nurse.*
> *One who is brought up with you.*
> *One who is an hereditary friend.*

Next, the qualities these friends should possess:

> *They should tell the truth.*
> *They should not change with time.*

The Male Lover

They should be favorable to your designs.
They should be firm.
They should be free from covetousness.
They should not be able to be gained over by others.
They should not reveal your secrets.

Finally, gallants should form friendships with the following persons: Washermen, barbers, cowherds, florists, druggists, betel-leaf sellers, tavern keepers, beggars, Pithamardas, Vitas, and Vidushkas. Gallants should also form friendships with the wives of these people, for these women will prove useful in their undertakings of love.

Vatsya Yana concludes that a *nayaka* "who is ingenious and wise, who is accompanied by a friend, and who knows the intentions of others, as well as the proper time and place for love, can quickly seduce even those women who are not easily won."

III
The Female Lover

III

THE
FEMALE
LOVER

In the Hindu philosophy of love, women are divided and subdivided into many more divisions than
men. As a matter of fact, the subdivisions are themselves subdivided endlessly by the finest shades of
classification. We shall not concern ourselves here

with insignificant trivialities but set forth only such groups as are distinct and pertinent to our purpose. It is not unnatural that women should be described in greater detail than men for it is the men who do the describing. Additionally, the Hindus assume, like all other eastern peoples, that women are incomparably more polymorphous than men.

We have seen that the male lover among the Hindus is called *nayaka*. The female prototype is correspondingly called the *nayika*. The Hindu idea of such a woman is one who is fit to be enjoyed without sin. As the object of enjoyment among them is two-fold—pleasure and progeny—any woman who can be enjoyed without sin for either of these purposes is considered a *nayika*.

Fundamentally, such women are classified according to social position. There are three distinct social types: maidens, women twice married, and legalized prostitutes. These three fundamental groups have been added to by various important eroticists and it may be worth while to mention some of these additional types. According to Gonikaputra there is a fourth class of *nayika*: the woman who is resorted to on some special occasion even though she be previously married to another. Charayana adds a fifth type: the woman who is kept by a minister or

who visits him sometimes, or a widow who serves
the purpose of a man with the person to whom she
resorts. Suvarnanabha adds that a woman who lives
as an ascetic after having been widowed may be considered a sixth kind of *nayika*. Ghotakamukha advances still another type: the daughter of a legalized
prostitute or a family servant, provided that she is
still a virgin. An eighth type is advanced by Gonardiya: the woman born of good family who is already
of age.

Vatsya Yana is somewhat contemptuous of this
intricate complexity and asserts that the last four
cases do not differ essentially from the fourth type.
This generic type is the *nayika* used on some particular occasion. Hence, generalizes Vatsya Yana,
there are only four distinct types: the maiden, the
twice married woman, the legalized prostitute, and
the woman resorted to for a special purpose.

There are some authoritative eroticists who in-
voke a fifth class: the eunuch. They regard him as
neither man nor woman in the physical embrace for
the pleasure of *auparishtaka* is peculiar to him alone.
For this reason these authorities regard him as a
special type of legalized prostitute, one who subserves as a preparation for further pleasure.

One of the most important ways of classifying

women is by the criterion of temperament. The Hindus group them into four divisions: the *padmini,* the *chitrini,* the *shankhini,* and the *hastini.* The description of these women by Kalyana Malla is most interesting from the peculiarly Hindu point of view and we quote it *in extenso:*

"She in whom the following signs and symptoms appear is called *padmini,* or lotus-woman (nervous temperament). Her face is pleasing as the full moon; her body, well clothed with flesh, is soft as the Shiras, that lofty tree with soft and fragrant pollen; her skin is fine, tender and fair as the yellow lotus, never dark-colored, though resembling in the effervescence and purple light of her youth, the cloud about to burst. Her eyes are bright and beautiful as the orbs of the fawn, well-cut, and with reddish corners. Her bosom is hard, full and high; her neck is goodly shaped as the conch shell, so delicate that the saliva can be seen through it; her nose is straight and lovely, and three folds or wrinkles cross her middle near the umbilical region. Her *yoni* resembles the opening lotus-bud, and her love-seed (*kama-salila*) is perfumed like the lily which has nearly burst. She walks with swan-like gait, and her voice is low and musical as the note of the Kokila bird (the nightingale of India); she delights in white raiment, in fine jewels, and in rich dresses. She eats little, sleeps lightly, and, being as respectable and religious as she is clever and courteous, she is ever anxious to worship the gods, and to enjoy the conversation of Brahmans. Such then, is the *padmini,* or lotus-woman.

"The *chitrini,* or art-woman (the sanguine temperament), is of the middle size, neither short nor tall, with bee-black hair, thin, round, shell-like neck; tender body; waist lean girthed as the lion's; hard, full breasts; well-turned thighs and heavily made hips. The hair is thin about the *yoni,* the mons veneris being soft, raised and round. The *kama-salila* is hot, and has the perfume of honey, producing from its abundance a sound during the embrace. Her eyes roll, and her walk is coquettish, like the swing of an elephant, whilst her voice is as excellent as that of the peacock. She is fond of pleasure and variety; she delights in singing and in every kind of accomplishment, especially the manual-arts; her carnal desires are not strong, and she loves her pets, parrots, mainas and other birds. Such is the *chitrini,* or art-woman.

"The *shankhini,* or conch-woman, is of bilious temperament, her skin being always hot and tawny, or dark yellow-brown; her body is large, her waist thick, and her breasts small; her head, hands and feet are thin and long, and she looks out of the corners of her eyes. Her *yoni* is ever moist with *kama-salila,* which is distinctly salty, and covered with thick hair. Her voice is hoarse and harsh, of the bass or contralto type; her gait is precipitate; she eats with moderation and she delights in clothes, flowers and ornaments of red color. She is subject to fits of amorous passion, which make her head ardent and her brain confused, and at the moment of enjoyment, she thrusts her nails into the flesh of her hus-band. She is of choleric constitution, hard-hearted, in-solent and vicious; irascible, rude, and ever addicted to finding fault. Such is the *shankhini,* or conch-woman.

"The *hastini* is short of stature; she has a stout coarse body, and her skin, if fair, is of a dead white; her hair is tawny, her lips are large; her voice is harsh, choked, and throaty and her neck is bent. Her gait is slow, and she walks in a slouching manner; often the toes of one foot are crooked. Her *kama-salila* has the savor of the juice which flows in spring from the elephants' temples. She is tardy in the Art of Love, and can be fulfilled only by prolonged congress, the longer the better, but it will never suffice her. She is gluttonous, shameless, and irascible. Such is the *hastini,* or elephant-woman."

Just as the male is divided into three classes ac-cording to length of *lingam,* so do the eroticists classify woman according to depth and extent of *yoni* into three groups: the *mrigi,* the deer-woman; the *vadava,* the mare-woman; the *karini,* or elephant-woman. Kalyana Malla in the *Ananga Ranga* affords us their detailed differences:

"The *mrigi* has a *yoni* six fingers deep. Her body is delicate, with girlish aspect, soft and tender. Her head is small and well-proportioned; her bosom stands up well; her stomach is thin and drawn in; her thighs and mons veneris are fleshy, and her build below the hips is solid, whilst her arms from the shoulder downwards are large and rounded. Her hair is thick and curly; her eyes are black as the dark lotus-flower; her nostrils are fine; her cheeks and ears are large; her hands, feet, and lower lip are ruddy, and her fingers are straight. Her voice is like that of the Kokila bird, and her gait the rolling of the elephant. She eats moderately, but is much addicted to the pleasures of love; she is affectionate but jealous, and she is active in mind when not subdued by her passions. Her *kama-salila* has the pleasant perfume of the lotus-flower.

"The *vadava* numbers nine fingers in depth. Her body is delicate; her arms are thick from the shoulders downwards; her breasts and hips are broad and fleshy, and her umbilical region is high-raised, but without protuberant stomach. Her hands and feet are red like flowers, and well proportioned. Her head slopes forwards and is covered with long and straight hair; her forehead is retreating; her neck is long and much bent; her throat, eyes, and mouth are broad, and her eyes are like the petals of the dark lotus. She has a graceful walk, and she loves sleep and good living. Though choleric and versatile, she is affectionate to her husband; she does not easily arrive at the height of enjoyment, and her *kama-salila* is perfumed like that of the lotus.

"The *karini* has a *yoni* twelve fingers in depth. Unclean in her person, she has large breasts; her nose, ears and throat are long and thick; her cheeks are blown or expanded; her lips are long and bent outwards; her eyes are fierce and yellow-tinged; her face is broad; her hair is thick and somewhat blackish; her feet, hands and arms are short and fat; and her teeth are large and sharp as a dog's. She is noisy when eating; her voice is hard and harsh; she is gluttonous in the extreme, and her joints crack with every movement. Of a wicked and utterly shameless disposition, she never hesitates to commit sin. Excited and disquieted by carnal desires, she is not easily satisfied, and requires congress unusually protracted. Her *kama-salila* is very abundant, and it suggests the juice which flows from the elephant's temples."

Kalyana Malla adds a word of caution to these exact words of description for well he knows the unquestioning credulity of the Hindu student. "The wise man will bear in mind that all these characteristics are not equally well defined, and their proportions can be known only by experience. Mostly the temperaments are mixed; often we find a combination of two and in some cases even of three. Great study, therefore, is required in judging by the absence or presence of the signs and symptoms, to choose the Chandrakala (the Calendar of Love) and other manipulations proper to the several differences, as without such judgment the consequences of congress are not satisfactory. Thus the student is warned that the several distinctions of the twelve combinations are seldom found without intermixture, and that it is his duty to learn the proportions in which they combine, and to act in accordance with his knowledge."

There are four periods in a woman's lifetime when she is ready for love. From eleven to sixteen years, she is called bala, prefers love in the darkness, and is quickly won by flowers, presents, and gifts of betel. From sixteen to thirty years, she is called taruni, prefers love in the light and is conquered by nothing less than gifts of dresses, pearls and ornaments. From thirty to fifty-five years, she is called praudha, enjoys love both in darkness and light but only on occasion, and easily submits to attention, politeness, kindness and love. Beyond fifty-five years she is called viddha, is unattractive to men, generally sick and infirm, and can always be seduced by flattery.

Another grouping of women, about which the Hindus are extremely serious, is based upon their previous state of existence. This is called the satva, or disposition inherited from a former life, and which influences their worldly natures. *Ratirahasya* numbers five; *Ananga Ranga* numbers nine; *Panca Sayaka* numbers four; and *Bharatiyanatya Shastra* as many as there are birds and animals in the world!

A representative list of these different characteristics follows and is far less disgusting to our western sense of morality than a complete list of unabridged qualities would be.

The Devasatva-stri belongs to the gods, is cheerful and lively, pure-bodied and clean, with perspiration perfumed like the lotus flower; she is clever, wealthy and industrious, of sweet speech and benevolent, always delighting in good works; her mind is sound as her body, nor is she ever tired of or displeased by her friends.

The Gandharvasatva-stri belongs to the heavenly minstrels, is beautiful of shape, patient in mind, delighting in purity, given to perfumes, fragrant substances and flowers, to singing and dancing, to rich dress and fair ornaments, to sport and amorous play, especially to the Vilasa, one of the classes of feminine actions which indicate the passion of love.

The Yakshasatva-stri belongs to the god of wealth, has large and fleshy breasts, with a skin fair as the white champa flower; she is fond of flesh and liquor, devoid of shame and decency, passionate and irascible, and at all hours greedy for congress.

The Munushyasatva-stri belongs to humanity, delights in the pleasures of friendship and hospitality; she is respectable and honest, her mind is free from guile, and she is never wearied of religious actions, vows and penances.

The Pisachasatva-stri belongs to a strange type of demons, has a short body, very dark and hot, with a forehead ever wrinkled; she is unclean in her person, greedy, fond of flesh and forbidden things, and, however much enjoyed, is ever eager of congress, like a harlot.

The Nagasatva-stri is the snake-woman, always in hurry and confusion; her eyes look drowsy, she yawns over and over again, and she sighs with deep-drawn breath, her mind is forgetful and she lives in doubt and suspicion.

The Kakasatva-stri has the characteristics of the crow, ever rolls her eyes as if in pain; throughout the whole day she wants food, she is silly, unhappy and unreasonable, spoiling everything she touches.

The Vanarasatva-stri has the characteristics of a monkey, rubs her eyes throughout the day, grinds and chatters with her teeth, and is very lively, active and mercurial.

The Kharasatva-stri has the characteristics of the ass, is unclean in her person, and avoids bathing, washing, and pure raiment; she cannot give a direct answer and speaks awkwardly and without reason because her mind is crooked.

The Hindu Art of Love

After these and other distinctions, Kalyana Malla adds three universal laws applying to certain types of women:

"The woman whose bosom is hard and fleshy, who appears short from the fullness of her frame, and looks bright and light colored, such an one is known to enjoy daily congress with her husband.

"The woman who, being thin, appears very tall and somewhat dark, whose limbs and body are languid, the effect of involuntary chastity, such an one suffers from long separation from her husband and from the want of conjugal embraces.

"A woman who eats twice as much as a man, is four times more reckless and wicked, six times more resolute and obstinate, and eight times more violent in carnal desire, such an one can hardly control her lust of congress, despite the shame and modesty which is natural to the sex."

We prefer not to weary the reader with further divisions which, like a geometric progression, serves as an outlet to the voluptuous imagination and philosophy of the Hindus. Above all things the reader must constantly bear in mind that the foundation not only of Hindu love but of all other aspects of Hindu life, rests upon these classifying niceties. Even the caste system, the sum and substance of

Hindu existence, is rooted inextricably upon this foundation.

To conclude this chapter on the *nayika*, we add the following suggestive description of women according to nationality. Very few of the important Hindu eroticists omit these geographical distinctions.

The woman of the Middle Region has red nails, but her body is even redder. She dresses well and in various sorts of apparel. She is an excellent housekeeper, perfectly broken to manual labor and other works, and much given to religious ceremonies. Though wonderfully fond of, and skillful in, amatory dalliance, she is averse to the tricks of teeth and nails (biting and scratching).

The Malwa woman likes to be enjoyed every day, and is well fitted for those who prefer the act of congress when long protracted. She is satisfied only by enduring embraces, which she greatly covets and desires, and sometimes the fingers must be employed for her paroxysm.

The woman of Mathra, Krishna's country, is fascinated by various forms of kissing. She delights in the closest embraces but has no tricks of tooth and nail.

The woman of Lata-Desha is delicate and handsome. She will dance with joy at the prospect of congress, and her movements of pleasure are frequent and violent. She is prompt in her embraces, and she may be moved also by softly biting her lips.

The woman of Telangana is so fascinating that she charms the stranger at first sight, and she is as sweet in voice as she is beautiful of body. She delights in jest and dalliance, yet is an utter stranger to shame, and is one of the most wicked of her sex.

The woman of Oude is very clever in the art of congress. She suffers much from prurience and titillation, and perpetually desires lengthened embraces of unusual vigor.

The woman of the Maratha country or Patalupta-Desha is fond of giving amorous side-glances, of dress and ornaments, of junketing and garden trips. Ever smiling gently, airy and gay, full of jest and sport and amorous dalliance, she is yet somewhat destitute of shame. Affectionate and coquettish, she is proficient in the toying of love.

The woman of Orissa is so beautiful that man is attracted to her at first sight, and her voice is soft as her body is delicate. She is loose and licentious, caring little for decency in her devotion to love, at which time she becomes violent, disquieted and excessively inflamed. She delights in different postures to vary enjoyment, and is easily satisfied, even by passing the fingers over her breasts.

The woman of Western Assam has a soft body and sweet voice; her affections are warm, and she is well skilled in all the arts of love. During congress she abounds in *kama-salila*.

The forest woman of the Bhills or other hill-tribes, has a stout body and healthy constitution. She delights, whilst concealing her own defects and blemishes, faults and follies, in exposing those of others.

The woman of Guzerat is wise and sensible. She has beautiful features, and eyes proportioned as they ought to be. She delights in handsome dresses and ornaments, and though warm and devoted to the pleasures of love, she is easily satisfied by short congress.

The woman of Sind, Punjab, or Bahawalpur has lively eyes, casting sidelong and amorous glances. She is volatile, irascible and wicked, and the fierceness, violence, and heat of her desires are very hard to satisfy.

The woman of Tirhoot has eyes blooming like the flowers of the lake; she loves her husband fondly and her passion is enflamed by a single look; she is especially skillful in congress; she enjoys various modes of embrace; and, by reason of her delicacy, she cannot endure caresses which are very rough or protracted.

The woman of Pushpapura, of Madda-desha, or of Tailanga-desha, though a proficient in the art of love, is modest and enjoys only her husband. Her form of passion is the Chanda-vega and her amorousness is excessive; she expresses delight by scratching, biting, patting, hair-handling, and other signs of ardent desire.

The woman of the Coromandel country, of Sauvira, or of Malayalim, is well proportioned in body and limbs, soft and delicate, and sweet of voice. She is satisfied with short congress, although fearless, shameless and headlong in wickedness.

The woman of Camboge or Paundra-desha is tall, robust and gross in body, and of wicked disposition; she is ignorant of the acts of congress accompanied by tricks of nail and tooth, and she is satisfied only by the violent embraces.

The woman of the mixed races, of Parvata, of Gandhara, or of Cashmere, is distinguished by evil savor of body. She is wholly ignorant of toying and dalliance, of kissing and caressing. She cares little for congress, and is easily satisfied by quick embraces.

The Female Lover

The Hindus all believe that only by study and experience of these women in different countries can the wise man learn to discern the diverse Chandrakalas, or preparatory caresses, which best suit races as well as individuals, and thus endear himself to womankind.

We do not elaborate this chapter on the *Female Lover* in conformity with the general tenor of this work which is to avoid every possible angle of obscenity. To enter into more intimate details therefore would be alien to our purpose.

IV

The Process and Practice of Love

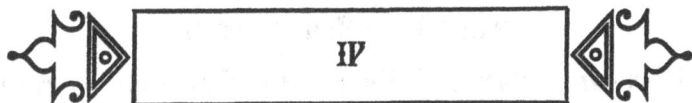

THE
PROCESS
AND
PRACTICE
OF
LOVE

We have already mentioned the Hindu belief that life has a three-fold goal, *purusartha*, as long as the individual does not yet wish release from the mortal coils of the world. If release, *Moksha*, is desired it is added as a fourth *purusartha* to the trinity—

Dharma, Artha and *Kama*. But this, save in rare instances, is little thought of before the arrival of ripe old age.

According to the accepted wisdom of the Hindus, man, whose normal life should last one hundred years, ought to practice *Dharma, Artha* and *Kama* at different times and in such a way that they combine harmoniously without clashing in any respect. He should acquire learning in his childhood; in his youth and middle age he should attend to Artha and Kama; and in his old age he should perform Dharma, and thus seek to gain Moksha, release from further transmigration. Or, on account of the uncertainty of life, he may practice them at such times as they are enjoined to be practiced. But one thing is to be noted: he should lead the life of a religious student until he finishes his education.

Dharma is obedience to the command of the *Shastra* or Holy Writ of the Hindus to fulfill certain duties, such as the performance of sacrifices, which are not generally obeyed, because they do not belong to this world, and produce no visible effect; and not to other duties, such as eating meat, which is often done because it belongs to this world, and has visible effects. Dharma should be learnt from the Holy Writ, and from those conversant with it.

The Process and Practice of Love

Artha is the acquisition of arts, land, gold, cattle, wealth, equipages, and friends. It is moreover the protection of what is acquired, and the increase of what is protected. Artha should be learnt from the king's officers, and from merchants well versed in the ways of commerce.

Kama is the enjoyment of appropriate objects by the five senses of hearing, feeling, seeing, tasting, and smelling, assisted by the mind together with the soul. The ingredient in this is a peculiar contact between the organ of sense and its object, and the consciousness of pleasure which arises from that contact is called Kama. Kama is to be learnt from the *Kama Sutra*, Aphorisms on Love, and from the behavior of citizens.

When all three, Dharma, Artha and Kama come together, they rank in the order named. Dharma is better than Artha, and Artha is better than Kama. But Artha should always be practised by the King, for the livelihood of men is to be obtained from it alone. Again, Kama being the occupation of public women, legalized prostitutes, they should prefer it to the other two; but these are exceptions to the general rule.

There are four chief Sanscrit synonyms for love. These are *kama, priti, sneha* and *shringara*. The

63

first signifies sexual love; the second, joy for the beloved object; the third, devotion, loyalty; the last, sexual love, as expressed emotionally in poetry, drama, etc.

On this point the *Kama Sutra* explains that men learned in the humanities are of the opinion that there are essentially only four classes of love of which men and women are capable:

1. *Love acquired by continual habit.*
2. *Love resulting from the imagination.*
3. *Love resulting from belief.*
4. *Love resulting from the perception of external objects.*

(1) Love resulting from the constant and continual performance of some act, is called love acquired by constant practice and habit, as for instance the love of sexual intercourse, the love of hunting, the love of drinking, the love of gambling, etc.

(2) Love of things to which we are not habituated, and which proceeds entirely from ideas, is called love resulting from the imagination, as for instance, that love which some men and women and eunuchs feel for the *Auparishtaka* or *cunnilingus,* and that which is felt for all such things as embracing, kissing, etc.

(3) Love which is mutual on both sides, and proved to be true, when each looks upon the other as his or her very own. Such is called love resulting from belief by the learned.

(4) Love resulting from the perception of external objects is obvious and well known to the world, because the pleasure which it affords is superior to the pleasure resulting from other kinds of love. The latter exist only to subserve this type of love.

Naturally enough, the Hindus further qualify the synonyms of love which are in themselves qualifications of the idea. The *Ananga Ranga*, for instance, represents four divisions of the *priti* connecting men with women:

1. Naisargiki priti is that natural affection by which husband and wife cleave to each other like the links of an iron chain. It is a friendship amongst the good of both sexes.

2. Vishaya priti is the fondness born in the woman, and increased by means of gifts, such as sweetmeats and delicacies, flowers, perfumery, and preparations of sandal-wood, musk, saffron, etc. It partakes therefore of gluttony, sensuality and luxury.

3. Sama priti is also sensual in proportion as it

65

arises from the equally urgent desires of both husband and wife.

4. Abhyasiki priti is the habitual love bred by mutual society. It is shown by walking in fields, gardens and similar places; by attending together at worship, penances and self-imposed religious observances; and by frequenting sportive assemblies, plays and dances, where music and similar arts are practised.

The rhetoricians have consumed endless rolls of parchment in discussions of the essence of love, the ideal, flowery kind not unlike European poesy. But intelligent Hindu students of love disdain such glittering generalities and confine themselves to the actual and sensual. For them sexual love is of the following kinds:

1. *Loving congress*
2. *Congress of subsequent love*
3. *Congress of artificial love*
4. *Congress of transferred love*
5. *Congress like that of the eunuchs*
6. *Deceitful congress*
7. *Congress of spontaneous love*

(1) When a man and woman who have been in love with each other for some time, come together

with great difficulty, or when one of the two returns from a journey, or is reconciled after having been separated on account of a quarrel, then congress is called the *loving congress*. It is carried on according to the desires of the lovers, and as long as they choose.

(2) When two persons come together, while their love for each other is still in its infancy, their congress is called the *congress of subsequent love*.

(3) When a man carries on the congress by exciting himself by means of any of the sixty-four methods, such as kissing, etc., or when a man and a woman come together, though in reality they are both attached to different persons, their congress is then called *congress of artificial love*. At this time all the ways and means mentioned in the *Kama Shastra* should be used.

(4) When a man, from the beginning to the end of the congress, thinks all the time that he is enjoying another woman whom he loves, it is called the *congress of transferred love*.

(5) Congress between a man and a female water-carrier or a female servant of a caste lower than his own, lasting only until the desire is satisfied, is called *congress like that of eunuchs*. Here external touches, kisses and manipulations are not to be employed.

(6) The congress between a prostitute and a rustic, or that between citizens and the women of villages and bordering countries, is called *deceitful congress*.

(7) The congress that takes place between two persons who are attached to one another, and which is done according to their own liking is called *spontaneous congress*.

A less categorical and probably more truthful classification of sexual love is found in Sarasvatikanthabharana and Sahityadarpana, who divide love into three branches:

1. *Legal*
2. *Commercial*
3. *Amorous*

We now reach a further method of division in the Hindu concept of sensual love. This covers the differences of degree as distinct from differences of kind, which a loving couple must pass through. Such descriptions are extremely numerous in Hindu literature.

These degrees of intensity in love are ten in number, and are distinguished by the following marks:

1. *Love of the eye*
2. *Attachment of the mind*

The Process and Practice of Love

3. *Constant reflection*
4. *Destruction of sleep*
5. *Emaciation of the body*
6. *Turning away from objects of enjoyment*
7. *Removal of shame*
8. *Madness*
9. *Fainting*
10. *Death*

These with exceptions too slight to mention, represent the basic degrees of love-longing. They are of incalculable importance because a man is theoretically permitted to commit adultery only when he finds himself passing from one stage or degree to another. This sidelight of Hindu love, directly contrary to Christian morality, is dealt with in the chapter on *The Paradox of Adultery*.

Gonikaputra sets down the general rule that a woman falls in love with every handsome man that she sees, and so does every man at the sight of a beautiful woman. Frequently, however, no further steps are taken to draw them closer together. The following conditions are peculiar to the woman in love. She loves without regard to right or wrong, and does not try to gain over a man simply for the attainment of some particular purpose. Moreover, when a man first makes up to her she naturally shrinks from him, even though she may be willing to unite herself with him. But when his attempts to gain her are repeated and renewed, she at last consents. With a man, however, even though he may have begun to love, he conquers his feelings out of regard for morality and wisdom, and although his thoughts are often on the woman, he does not yield, despite any attempt made to gain him over. He sometimes attempts to win the object of his affections, and having failed, he leaves her alone for the future. In the same way, when a woman is once gained, he often becomes indifferent about her. As for the saying that a man does not care for women who are easily won, but desires only such as can be conquered with difficulty, that is a "matter of talk."

The following are the signs by which wise eroticists know that a woman is amorous: She rubs and repeatedly smooths her hair to make it look well. She scratches her head so that notice may be drawn to it. She strokes her own cheeks so as to entice her husband. She draws her dress over her bosom, apparently to readjust it, but leaves her breasts partly exposed. She bites her lower lip as if chewing it. At times she looks ashamed without cause as the result of her own ardent fancies, and sits quietly in the corner, engrossed with her reveries of sexual lust. She embraces her female friends, laughing loudly and speaking sweet words, with wit and jests. She kisses and hugs young children, especially boys. She smiles with one cheek, loiters, and unnecessarily stretches herself under some pretence or other. At times she looks at her shoulders and under her arms. She stammers and does not speak clearly and distinctly. She sighs and sobs without reason, and she yawns whenever she wants tobacco, food or sleep. She may even at the height of her passion throw herself in her beloved's way and is not easily persuaded to remove herself.

A woman may reject a man for the following reasons: affection for her husband; desire of lawful progeny; want of opportunity; anger at being addressed by the man too familiarly; difference in rank of life; want of certainty due to the man's frequent travels; the thought that the man may be attached to some other person; fear of the man's failure of keeping his attentions secret; the thought that the man is too devoted to his friends and has too great regard for them; the apprehension that he is not in earnest; bashfulness when he is an illustrious man; fear when he is powerful, or possessed of a too impetuous passion (in the case of the deer-woman); bashfulness on account of his being too clever; the thought of having once lived with him only on friendly terms; contempt for his lack of worldly wisdom; distrust of his low character; disgust with his blindness of her love; the thought that he is a man of weak passion and potency (in the case of the elephant-woman); compassion lest anything might befall him on account of his passion; despair at her own imperfections; fear of discovery; disillusion at seeing his grey hair or shabby appearance; fear that he may be employed by her husband to test her chastity; the fear that he has too much regard for morality.

If the man is at first unsuccessful in his advances to the woman, he should try and find out to which of the above causes it may be due. He should then try his best to immediately remove the hindrance. He should subdue her bashfulness arising from his reputation by manifesting his affection for her. He should remove the excessive respect of the woman for him by making himself very familiar. He should show his valor or wisdom by dispelling any ideas of his lowness. He should prove his prowess in love if she fears that he is a man of little passion by a recital of his potency by himself or by others.

Three subjects are all-important in the study of the Science of Love. First, the kinds of men who are usually successful in obtaining the love of women: men well versed in the Science of Love; men skilled in telling stories; men acquainted with women from their childhood; men who have secured their confidence; men who send presents to them; men who talk well; men who do the things that they like; men who have not loved other women previously; men who act as messengers; men who know women's weak points; men who are desired by good women; men who are united with their female friends; men who are good-looking; men who have been brought up with them; men who are their neighbors; men who are devoted to sexual pleasures; men who are the lovers of their daughters' nurse; men who have been lately married; men who like picnics and pleasure parties; men who are generous; men who are celebrated for their potency; men who are enterprising and brave; men who surpass their husbands in learning and good looks, in good qualities, and in liberality; and men who dress and live in a magnificent manner.

Second, the women who can be easily won over to congress: women who stand at the door of their houses; women who are always looking out on the street; women who sit conversing in their neighbor's house; a woman who is always staring at you; a female messenger; a woman who looks sideways at you; a woman whose husband has taken another wife without any just cause; a woman who hates her husband, or who is hated by him; a woman who has nobody to look after her, or keep her in check; a woman who has not had any children; a woman whose family or caste is not well known; a woman whose children are dead; a woman who is very fond of society; a woman who is apparently very affectionate toward her husband; the wife of an actor; a widow; a poor woman; a woman fond of enjoyments; the wife of a man with many younger brothers; a vain woman; a woman whose husband is inferior to her in rank or ability; a woman who is proud of her skill in the arts; a woman disturbed in mind by the folly of her husband; a woman who has been married in her infancy to a rich man and who desires at her maturity a man more suitable to her own tastes; a woman who is slighted by her husband without cause; a woman who is not respected by other women of the same rank or beauty as herself; a woman whose husband is devoted to travelling; the wife of a jeweller; a jealous woman; a covetous woman; an immoral woman; a barren woman; a lazy woman; a cowardly woman; a humpbacked woman; a dwarfish woman; a deformed woman; a vulgar woman; an ill-smelling woman; a sick woman; and an old woman.

Third, the periods when women have the greatest desire for congress and when they are most easily satisfied and subjected by men, are the following: When tired by walking and exhausted by bodily exercise; after a long want of intercourse; a month after childbirth; during the earlier stages of pregnancy; when dull, idle and sleepy; if recently cured of fever; when showing signs of wantonness or bashfulness; when feeling unusually merry and happy; immediately before and after the menstruals; maidens enjoyed for the first time; throughout the spring season; during thunder, lightning and rain.

We now proceed to the method of the Hindus in carrying out love-affairs. The acknowledged procedure between two parties is quite simply set forth: The lover is introduced to the woman by a mutual friend or on a special occasion. He gives her hints of his love and if he finds from her replies that she receives these hints favorably, he should immediately set to work to seduce her without any fear. If the woman manifests her love by outward signs to the man at his first interview, he should feel no hesitancy in obtaining his aims. Similarly, a lascivious woman who, when addressed in loving words, replies openly expressing her love, is a most compliant victim. In general, the eroticists set down one rule for the use of man in regard to all women, be they wise, simple or confiding: Make an immediate and open manifestation of love. If they will, they will; if they won't, they can be induced to. There is no reason for lost time in the first case; in the second, it is well to understand your position and to proceed from that point according to directions already stated, as well as by later instruction in the following chapters.

Naturally, in practice the procedure is more complex and detailed. First of all, the acquaintance of the woman should be made in one of the following manners: the man should arrange a natural opportunity to be seen by the woman, one visiting the house of the other; or by a special opportunity, meeting at the house of a mutual friend or at a public occasion.

Whatever the meeting, the man should be careful to look at her in such a way that his state of mind immediately becomes known to her. He should pull at his mustache, create a sound with his nails, bite his lower lip, tinkle his ornaments, and provoke various other signs of that nature. When she is looking at him he should speak to his friends about her and other women, and should show her his liberality and his appreciation of enjoyments. When sitting by the side of a female friend he should yawn and twist his body, contract his eyebrows, speak very slowly as if weary, and listen to her indifferently.

A conversation of *double entendre* should also be carried on with a child or some other person, apparently with regard to a third person, but really referring to the woman he loves. In this way his love should be made manifest under the pretext of referring to others rather than to herself.

If a child is sitting in the woman's lap, he should give it something to play with and converse with her about the youngster. In this manner he gradually becomes acquainted with her, and he should also make himself agreeable to her relations. This acquaintance should be used as a pretext of visiting her house frequently, and on such occasions he should talk on the subject of love, not to her directly but within her hearing.

As his intimacy with her increases he should place in her charge some kind of deposit or trust and regularly remove small portions of it. Afterwards, he should endeavor to acquaint her with his own wife, and get them to carry on confidential conversations, and to sit together in lonely places. He should also pay her long visits under the pretence of being engaged with her on business, and one business should lead to another, in order to maintain their intercourse.

Whenever she wants anything, or is in need of money, or wishes to acquire skill in one of the arts, he should lead her to believe that he is willing and able to do anything she chooses, to give her money or to teach her one of the arts, for all these things are quite within his ability and power. Similarly, he should hold discussions with her in company with other people and if she begins to dispute with him and other people he should not contradict her, but pretend that he agrees with her in every respect.

The man now breaks ground and brings the affair to a declaration. If she listens to him, but does not manifest in any way her own intentions, he should then try to win her by means of a procuress or go-between. This not uncommon type of female messenger is discussed in the chapter on *The Role of the Procuress*.

But if she meets him once, and again comes to meet him better dressed than before, or comes to him in some lonely place, he should be certain that she is capable of being enjoyed by the use of a little force. If the woman lets the man make up to her, but does not give herself even after a long time, she should be considered as a trifler in love. Nevertheless, owing to the fickleness of the woman's mind she can be conquered if a close acquaintanceship is kept up with her and the first opportunity seized.

When a woman avoids the attention of a man and, on account of respect for him and pride in herself, can be possessed only with extreme difficulty, a clever procuress will prove of excellent aid in breaking down her resistance.

When a man makes up to a woman and she reproaches him with harsh words, waste no time with her. When a woman reproaches a man but at the same time acts affectionately towards him, she should be made love to in every way for she will be certain to give in.

The following is the most common case and consequently the eroticists describe it in full detail. A woman who meets a man in a lonely place and puts up with the touch of his leg but pretends not to be aware of it can be conquered by patience: if she happens to go to sleep within his observation he should put his left arm around her and see when she awakens whether she repulses him genuinely, or merely repulses him in such a way as to invite a repetition of the same embrace. And what is done by the arm can also be done by the leg. If a man succeeds in this point he should embrace her more closely and if she will not tolerate the embrace and gets up, but behaves with him as usual the next day, he should know then that she is not unwilling to be enjoyed by him.

A man should proceed to enjoy any woman when she gives him an opportunity and makes her own love manifest to him by the following signs: she calls out to a man without first being addressed by him; she shows herself to him in secret places; she speaks to him tremblingly and inarticulately; her face blooms with delight and her fingers or toes perspire; and sometimes she remains with both hands placed on his body as if she had been surprised by something, or as if overcome with fatigue.

After a woman has manifested her love to him by outward signs, and by the motions of her body, the man should make every possible attempt to conquer her. There should be no indecision or hesitancy: if an opening is found the man should make the most of it. The woman, indeed, becomes disgusted with the man if he is timid about his chances and throws them away. Boldness is the rule, for everything is to be gained, and nothing lost.

The following words of advice are deemed necessary by the classic eroticists: when a man is endeavoring to seduce one woman, he should not attempt to seduce another at the same time. But after he has succeeded with the first, and enjoyed her for a considerable time, he can keep her affections by occasionally giving her small gifts, and then commence making up to another woman. A wise man, having a regard for his reputation, should not think of seducing a woman who is apprehensive, timid, untrustworthy, well guarded, or one who has a watchful father-in-law or mother-in-law.

From all these counsels on seduction it is quite evident that the act of seduction *per se* is not held in an immoral light among the Hindus. It is because of this attitude and many another similar mode of conduct, as we shall gather from further reading, that the Hindu is able to build his complex structure of an unequalled Art of Love. If the vagrant nature of the Hindu were more controlled by spiritual motives, his Art of Love could be neither so complex nor so basically immoral.

V

The Calendar of Love

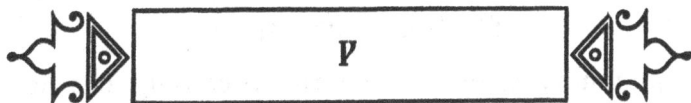

THE
CALENDAR
OF
LOVE

Although Hindu eroticism is unimaginably rich in all the byways and crossways of genesic impulse, the Calendar of Love is supremely unique and represents perhaps the major triumph of Hindu voluptuousness. The reader may not have recovered his equanimity after reading the preceding chapters with their manifold *minutiæ* of detail. What then will be his amazement at the tables presented in this chapter! The inevitable question will thrust itself whether the Hindus can actually believe in these doctrines, and if so, can they follow them strictly.

A word or two of explanatory reply. It was not until comparatively recent years that Europe and America discovered the simple fact that the most excitable period in women occurs directly before and after menstruation. Furthermore, that conception takes place most easily during this period. We know little more than these facts about the periodic passion of women but the ancient Hindus knew this and much more. They discovered and promulgated laws covering not only the months of the year, and the days of the month, but even the hours of the day when women were most easily subject to sexual stimulation. Nor was this all. They sought to discover the various erogenous zones of women and the most suitable means for their excitation and enjoyment.

These facts were rather late developments among the Hindus. The earlier classics like the *Kama Sutra* make no mention of the tithis, or lunar days, and the chandrakalas, or phases of the moon, and their corresponding effects upon the passions of women. It is only in later classics such as the *Ratirahasya, Ananga Ranga, Panca Sayaka,* and *Smara Dipika* that the subject is discussed at some length. Kalyana Malla, for instance, sets down a table illustrating what days each type of women derives the greatest pleasure from congress. According to the poet, who would have every nayaka learn this table by heart, no amount of congress will satisfy the passions of women unless practised on the days specified.

TABLE I

Pratipada 1st day	Dvitya 2nd day	Chaturthi 4th day	Panchami 5th day
Satisfy the Padmini			

Shashati 6th day	Ashtami 8th day	Dashami 10th day	Dwadashi 12th day
Satisfy the Chitrini			

Tritiya 3rd day	Saptami 7th day	Ekadashi 11th day	Trayodasi 13th day
Satisfy the Shankhini			

Navami 9th day	Chaturdashi 14th day	Purnima Full Moon	Amavasya New Moon
Satisfy the Hastini			

The Hindu Art of Love

We have previously observed that the four distinct types of women prefer different periods for congress. The padmini derives no satisfaction from nocturnal congress but, like the day-lotus which opens its eyes to the sun only, will readily surrender herself during the bright hours of day. The chitrini and the shankhini, on the other hand, resemble the night-lotus which expands to the cooling rays of the moon. They avoid the embrace by day and receive satisfaction only during the dark. The hastini, who as we have already seen is the coarsest of all women, ignores these delicate distinctions and knows no preference of day or night. These distinctions, like ever so many others, are tabulated by the eroticists for ambitious students who would master every refinement of the art of love which are within the wide limits of Hindu morality.

All the authorities discuss the erogenous zones of women and prescribe various preparatory caresses for the different zones in order to heighten pleasure and satisfaction. Of course, every caress must have its appropriate time in the lunar cycle and must correspond to some particular part of the woman's person. If any divergence from any one of these three elements takes place neither sex will be thoroughly satisfied. Indeed, such a mistake would inevitably lead, so say the eroticists, to adulteries of all sorts and these adulteries in turn would lead to quarrels, murders, and other deadly sins. Therefore, to avoid such catastrophes, one must study and master the chandrakala.

Passion resides in the woman's right side during the shuklapksha, the first or light fortnight of the lunar month, from new moon to full, including the fifteenth day. The reverse is the case on the dark fortnight, including its first day, and lasting from the full to the new moon. The shifting is supposed to take place by the action of light and darkness, otherwise the site of passion would be one and the same. These details are clarified in Table II on the following page.

These particulars are not detailed enough for the Hindu lover for he must differentiate the four distinct types of womanhood. Once these generalized differences are understood, the nayaka must learn in what member or part of body the woman's passion resides and by what type of caress it can be satisfied. It is immoral for the nayaka to continue after the two tell-tale signs of complete gratification are observed. These signs are the bristling of the body-hair and the utterance of the sitkara. The latter is the inarticulate sound produced by breathing hard

The Hindu Art of Love

TABLE II

SHUKLAPAKSHA: light fortnight, right side		THE TOUCHES BY WHICH PASSION IS SATISFIED	KRISHNAPAKSHA: dark fortnight, left side	
Day	Place		Place	Day
15	Head and hair	Hold hair, and caress the head with fingertips	Head and hair	1
14	Right eye	Kiss and fondle	Left eye	2
13	Lower lip	Kiss, bite and chew	Upper lip	3
12	Right cheek	Kiss, bite and chew	Left cheek	4
11	Throat	Scratch gently with nails	Throat	5
10	Side	Scratch gently with nails	Side	6
9	Breasts	Hold in hand and gently knead	Breasts	7
8	All the Bosom	Tap softly with base of fist	All the Bosom	8
7	Navel	Pat softly with open palm	Navel	9
6	Back	Hold, squeeze and tap with fist	Back	10
5	Thigh	Stroke gently	Thigh	11
4	Knee	Press with application of knee and fillip with finger	Knee	12
3	Calf of leg	Press with application of calf and fillip with finger	Calf of leg	13
2	Foot	Press with toe, and thrust the latter	Foot	14
1	Big toe	Press with toe, and thrust the latter	Big toe	15

The Calendar of Love

and drawing in the air between the closed teeth, and derives its name from the sibilant *s't, s't.*

Naturally enough, there is a table of these preliminary embraces to congress for each of the four classes of women. These tables are so astonishing in their thoroughness that the serious reader of this work will hardly keep from wondering if the Hindu lover was able to memorize them all. Even if he had memorized them, one imagines that he would have forgotten just which type of caress to bestow on any particular limb under the stress and struggle of passion. And if his memory was not sufficiently retentive, did he take the tables to bed with him?

We present on the next page the table of the padmini, the day-lotus woman possessed of a nervous temperament. There are similar tables for the chitrini, the shankhini, and the hastini, but we do not append them in this volume because they are essentially analogous despite their diversity of detail.

What immodesty! the casual reader exclaims. But this indicates a total misunderstanding of the Hindu theory of love. Man is the focal point of love. He must undertake every possible means of completely satisfying the woman. He must be familiar with all the possible signs and symbols expressing her likes

The Hindu Art of Love

TABLE III

Member	First Day	Second Day	Fourth Day	Fifth Day
Throat	Hug with force	Hug with force	Hug with force	Hug with force
Cheek	Kiss and scratch	Kiss and scratch	Kiss and scratch	Kiss and scratch
Hair	Stroke slowly with right hand	Stroke slowly with right hand	Stroke slowly with right hand	Stroke slowly with right hand
Waist	Apply nails and scratch	Apply nails and scratch	Apply nails and scratch	Apply nails and scratch
Breast	Scratch gently	Scratch gently	Scratch gently	Scratch gently
Back	Scratch and tap with fist	Scratch and tap with fist	Scratch and tap with fist	Scratch and tap with fist
Bosom	Press with nails	Press with nails	Squeeze and knead	Press and rub
Side	Scratch and press with nails	Scratch and press with nails	Scratch and press with nails	Scratch and press with nails
Thigh	Scratch and press with nails	Scratch and press with nails	Scratch and press with nails	Scratch and press with nails
Belly	Scratch and press with nails	Scratch and press with nails	Scratch and press with nails	Scratch and press with nails
Arm	Scratch and press with nails	Scratch and press with nails	Jerk suddenly and twitch	Jerk suddenly and twitch
Lip	Bite softly and kiss	Kiss	Bite softly and suck	Bite softly
Nipple	Bite softly and kiss	Bite softly and kiss	Bite softly and kiss	Kiss and pinch softly
Space between eyes	Kiss	Kiss	Kiss	Kiss
Foot	Scratch and press with nails	Scratch and press with nails	Scratch and press with nails	Scratch and press with nails

and dislikes. Granted that such a localization of passion borders upon vulgarity, yet it has a noteworthy feature, almost wholly unknown to our civilization. The man, by such experimentation, learns to know the woman and her moods thoroughly and does not treat her as a mere animal for the satisfaction of his sexual desires alone. The European, like the American, commences and quickly terminates the embrace, then turns over on his side and goes to sleep, totally disregarding his partner's feelings. This conduct would seem altogether incomprehensible to the Hindus. The basis of the Calendar of Love is that it thoroughly prepares the woman for congress and gives her varied and complete satisfaction. In the following chapters we shall see that the Hindus are essentially pragmatic in their doctrines even if intemperate in their behavior.

VI

Preliminaries to Possession

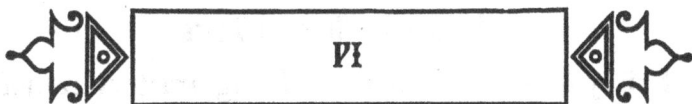

PRELIMINARIES
TO
POSSESSION

We have already observed that there are sixty-four social arts which a man must learn before he is fit to become a lover. But these social assets are not sufficient in themselves. In addition to these requirements, he must be practised in a further series of sixty-four arts, this series being amatory rather than social. These amatory arts or preliminaries to possession comprise in reality the entire Hindu Theory and Practise of Caresses.

The first great province of the caress—we use the generic term *caress* to include all preparatory love-toying, tousling, and dalliance—is the embrace. Under this head are distinguished four kinds: touching, piercing, rubbing, pressing.

When by some pretext a man walks in front or alongside of a woman and touches her body with his own, students of love call this the *touching embrace*.

When a woman bends down as if to pick up something and with her breasts seems to pierce a man, sitting or standing, and the man in turn takes hold of her breasts, students of love call this the *piercing embrace*.

When two lovers are walking slowly together in the dark, in a lonely place or during a festival, and rub their bodies against each other, students of love call this the *rubbing embrace*.

If however one of them presses the other's body forcibly against a wall or pillar, students of love call this the *pressing embrace*.

The first two of these embraces take place when the couple are as yet ignorant of the intentions of each other and use these methods of discovering them. The last two take place when the couple are aware of each other's intentions and employ these methods of satisfying them.

There are four additional embraces possible between lovers: the twining of a creeper, the climbing of a tree, the mixture of sesamum-seed with rice, and the milk and water embrace.

The woman clings to the man as a creeper twines round a tree, clings to his waist, kissing him softly until he draws in his breath while she softly makes the sound of sitkara. This is called by students of love *embracing as the creeper twines about the tree.*

The woman places her naked feet on the man's and encircling his waist with her arms, as if to climb up to receive a kiss. This is called by students of love the *embrace which simulates the climbing of a tree.*

The two lovers embrace by mutually encircling the waist. This is called by students of love the *embrace which represents the mixture of sesamum-seed with rice.*

The lovers closely embrace each other, their arms and legs entangled. This is called the *milk and water embrace.*

The above embraces are minutely described in

Sanscrit but here, as everywhere else in this volume, we omit too minute exactitude of detail as unnecessarily suggestive.

Finally, there are four further ways of embracing: thighs, navel, breasts, and forehead.

In the *embrace of the thighs* both lovers stand up, passing their arms round each other, and entwine their thighs.

In the *embrace of the navels* the man sits cross-legged upon the carpet and the woman upon his thighs, embracing and kissing him with fond affection. The man may also for variety's sake sit in the woman's lap.

In the *embrace of the breasts* the man sits still, closing his eyes, and the woman, placing herself close to him, passes her right arm over his shoulder and applies her bosom to his, pressing him tightly, whilst he returns her embrace with equal warmth.

In the *embrace of the foreheads* great endearment is shown by the close pressure of arms round the waist, both lovers standing upright, and by the contact of brow, cheek, eye and mouth.

Vatsya Yana quotes some verses on this section: "The whole subject of embracing is of such a nature that men who ask questions about it, or who hear about it, or who talk about it, acquire thereby a desire for enjoyment. Even those embraces that are not mentioned in the *Kama Shastra* should be practised at the time of sexual enjoyment, if they are in any way conducive to love or passion. The rules of the *Shastra* apply so long as the passion of man is middling, but when the wheel of love is once set in motion, there is then no *Shastra* and no order."

After the embrace, the second great province of the caress is *kissing*. The different modes of the kiss should be applied at the same time as the *embrace*. In general, the following places are held kissable: the lips, eyes, cheeks, head, throat, bosom, breasts and the interior of the mouth. Less common is the kissing of the arm-pit, navel and the pubic region, but these are not certified by the eroticists who consider them due to base passions by voluptuaries of hot countries.

First, there are three kinds of "acquaintance" kisses: nominal, throbbing, and touching.

When a girl merely touches the mouth of her lover with her own and does nothing else; or, if she is angry and will not kiss him, and he forcibly fixes his lips on hers and keeps both mouths united till her ill-temper has passed away, this is called by students of love the *nominal kiss*.

When a girl sets aside her bashfulness and wishes

to touch the lip that is pressed into her mouth and so moves only her lower lip, this is called, by students of love, the *throbbing kiss*.

When a girl touches her lover's lip with her tongue, shuts her eyes, places her hands on those of her lover; when she is excited with passion, covers his eyes with her hands and, closing her own, thrusts her tongue into his mouth, moving it to and fro so slowly that it suggests a higher form of enjoyment, this is called by students of love the *touching kiss*.

Kisses may be also straight, turned, and pressed, according to the positions of the mouths of the lovers. There is also a variant of the last, the *greatly pressed kiss:* the lower lip is held between two fingers, touched with the tongue and then pressed with great force by the other's lip.

Furthermore, kissing is of four kinds: moderate, contracted, pressed, and soft, according to the part of the body being kissed since certain parts require more pressure and duration.

Other kisses are: the kiss of the upper lip (only the upper lip of each of the lovers is kissed); the clasping kiss (the lips of one are between the lips of the other); the kiss that kindles love (the woman kisses the sleeping lover to awaken him to combat); the kiss that turns away (the woman distracts her lover's attention from any problem not connected with love, and brings him back to his proper work); the kiss that awakens (the lover coming home late at night to his beloved, fixes his lips on hers and gradually increases the pressure till she awakens and is ready for him); the kiss showing the intention (the lover apprises his beloved of his intentions by kissing her reflection in the mirror, picture or water); the transferred kiss (the lover kisses a child or image in the presence of his beloved); the demonstrative kiss (the lover kisses some part of the woman's body or dress to apprise her of his intentions).

Kissing games are of course commonly played among the Hindus. Vatsya Yana tells of a well-known diversion between passionate lovers: "A wager is laid as to which will first get hold of the lips of the other. If the woman loses, she pretends to cry, keeps her lover off by shaking her hands, and turns away from him, saying, 'Let another wager be laid.' If she loses a second time, she appears doubly distressed, and when her lover is off his guard or asleep, she gets hold of his lower lip, holding it in her teeth so that it should not slip away, and then laughs, making a loud noise, deriding him, dancing about, moving her eyebrows and rolling her eyes."

The Hindu Art of Love

After embracing and kissing, the third great province of the caress is *scratching*: pressing, marking, and scratching with the nails. Authorities differ on the proper occasions for this form of caress but agree that it is advisable at the following times: when a woman is angry or intoxicated; when first enjoying a woman or when deflowering a virgin; when separating for a short time; when departing for a foreign country; on returning from a journey; when a great pecuniary loss has been sustained; and when excited with desire for congress.

Pressure may be exerted on the following parts: neck, hands, thighs, breasts, back, sides, shoulders, bosom, hips, forearms and armpits, and both the cheeks.

The nails should be bright, well set, clean, entire, convex, soft and glossy. Wise men have given in the Shastras these qualities of the nails.

The following are the types of scratches:

When a person presses the cheeks, breasts, or lower lip of another so softly that no scratch or mark is left, but only the body-hair bristles from the touch of the nails, and the nails themselves make a sound, it is called a sounding or pressing with the nails.

The curved mark with the nails which is impressed on the neck and the breasts is called the half-moon.

Preliminaries to Possession

When the half-moons are impressed opposite to each other, it is called a circle. This mark with the nails is generally made on the navel, the small cavities about the nates, and on the joints of the thighs.

A mark in the form of a small thread which can be made on any part of the body is called a line.

This same line when curved and on the breast is called a tiger's claw.

When a curved mark is made on the breast by means of the five nails, it is called a peacock's foot. This is made by placing the thumb upon the nipple, and the four fingers upon the breast adjacent, and requires a great deal of skill.

When five marks with the nails are made close to one another near the nipple of the breast, it is called the hopping of the hare.

A mark made on the breast or on the hips in the shape of that type of leaf is called the leaf of a blue lotus.

When a person leaves for a journey and makes a mark on the thighs or on the breast, it is called a token of remembrance.

Kalyana Malla declares: "The voluptuary, by applying the nails as directed with love and affection, and driven wild by the fury of passion, affords the greatest comfort to the sexual desires of the woman; in fact, there is nothing perhaps more delightful to lovers than the science of unguiculation."

Inasmuch as in ancient times the breasts of women were not covered, it was not considered a disgrace to be seen with nail markings on the bosom. Vatsya Yana declares that when a stranger observes a young woman with the marks of nails on her breast, he is filled with love and respect for her.

After embracing, kissing, and scratching, the fourth great province of the caress is *biting*. Any spot that may be kissed, may be bitten, with the exception of the upper lip, the interior of the mouth, and the eyes. The teeth preferred in a lover are those whose color is somewhat rosy and not dead white, bright and clean, strong, pointed, short, and forming close regular rows.

The following are the successive categories of biting: secret biting (applying the teeth only to the inner part of the woman's lips, leaving no outside mark); simple biting (biting of any part of the woman's lips or cheeks); coral biting (the union of the man's teeth and the woman's lips); drop-biting (the mark left by the husband's two front teeth upon the woman's lower lip); rosary biting (the employment of all the front teeth); cluster biting (the prints of the lover's teeth upon the brow and cheek, the neck and breast of his beloved); biting of the boar (the deep and lasting marks left on the body of a woman in the heat of passion); the line of jewels (marks left by biting with all the teeth).

According to various classicists, when a nayaka bites a woman forcibly, she should angrily do the same to him with double force. The coral should be returned by drop biting, the rosary by the cluster, and so forth. If the woman is excessively chafed, she should start a love quarrel. She should take hold of her lover by the hair, bend his head down, and kiss his upper lip; then, intoxicated with love, she should shut her eyes and bite him in various places. Even by day, and in a place of public resort, when her lover points out any mark which she may have inflicted on his body, she should smile at the sight of it, and, turning her face as if to chide him, should show him with an angry grimace the marks on her own body that have been made by him.

After embracing, kissing, scratching and biting, the fifth great province of the caress is hair-handling. The woman's hair should be soft, close, thick, black, and wavy, neither kinky nor straight. According to the Kalyana Malla (this division is lacking in the *Kama Sutra*) "one of the best ways of kindling ardent desire in a woman is, at the time of her rising, softly to hold and handle her hair, according to the manner laid down in the *Kama Shastra*."

There are four divisions of hair-handling:

Holding the hair with both hands: the lover or husband encloses the hair between his two palms behind his beloved's head, at the same time kissing her lower lip.

Kissing the hair in a wavy fashion: the lover draws his beloved towards him by the back hair, and kisses her at the same time.

The dragon's turn: the lover, excited by the approaching prospect of congress, amorously seizes the hind knot of his beloved's hair, at the same time closely embracing her.

Holding the crest-hair of love: the lover during congress holds with both his hands his wife's hair above her ears, while she does the same to him, and both exchange frequent kisses upon the mouth.

After embracing, kissing, scratching, biting, and hair-handling the sixth great province of the caress is patting. Our English phrase, love-taps, receives an unexpected and startling confirmation from the Hindu eroticists who discourse learnedly on when, where, and how a nayaka may strike his nayika. But, asks Yashodara, blows create hatred: how then can they be conducive to love? His master, Vatsya Yana, answers: "Sexual congress may be compared to a quarrel, on account of the contrarieties of love and its tendency to dispute." Kalyana Malla similarly declares: "The blandishments of love are a kind of battle, in which the stronger wins the day. And in order to assist us in the struggle, we have certain forms of attack." The reader should note that this province of the caress does not denote brutal beatings but rather soft tappings by the husband and wife, or the lover and beloved. There is no hint here of flagellation or the grimmer aspects of sexual brutality which we call sadism.

The Hindu lover uses four types of patting on the woman: patting with the open palm on the flesh below the ribs and the pubic vicinity; patting with the back of the hand on bosom and breasts; striking gently with the lower or fleshy part of the closed hand on the back and hip; patting with the inner part of the hand, slightly hollowed for the purpose, the head of the beloved.

Similarly, there are four corresponding caresses practised by the woman on the lover: gently patting with the closed fist her lover's breast when the two have become one, so as to increase his pleasure; gently patting her lover during congress with the open hand; filliping her lover's body during congress with the thumbs only; the woman filliping her lover's body during congress with thumb and forefinger only.

After embracing, kissing, scratching, biting, hairhandling, and patting, the seventh great province of the caress is sighing. These inarticulate sounds, produced by drawing in the breath between the closed teeth, are the peculiar privilege and prerogative of women in the intimacies of love and passion.

Vatsya Yana names eight kinds of sighs: the sound Hin; the thundering sound; the cooing sound; the weeping sound; the sound Phut; the sound Phat; the sound Sut; and the sound Plat. He adds that "blows with the fist should be given on the back of the woman, sitting on the lap of the man, and she should give blows in return, abusing the man as if she were angry, and making the cooing and the weeping sounds. While the woman is engaged in congress the space between the breasts should be struck with the back of the hand, slowly at first, and then in proportion to the increasing excitement, until the end."

Kalyana Malla, on the other hand, agrees with other eroticists in presenting only five distinct lovesighings, each of which is similar to the cry of a bird indigenous to India. "These sounds," he explains,

Preliminaries to Possession

"should especially be produced by the woman when her husband or lover kisses, bites, and chews her lower lip. The sweetness of the utterance greatly promotes the mutual enjoyment." According to Kalyana Malla, these five love-cries are:

The deep and grave sound, like hun! hun! hun! Hin! hin! hin! produced in the nose and mouth with the slightest use of the former member.

The low rumbling, like the distant thunder, expressed by ha! ha! or by han! han! han! produced by the throat without the concurrence of the nasal muscles.

The expiration or emission of breath, like the hissing of the serpent, expressed by shan! shan! shan! or shish! shish! and produced only in the mouth.

The cracking sound, resembling the splitting of the bamboo, expressed by t'hat! t'hat! and formed by applying the tongue-tip to the palate, and by moving it as rapidly as possible, at the same time pronouncing the interjection.

The rattling sound, like the fall of heavy rain-drops, expressed by t'hap! t'hap! produced by the lips; but it can be produced only at the time of congress.

Enough. We spare the American reader further

111

manifestations of the caress as practised by the tire-
less Hindus. There are indeed many others though
none so well known and popular as the foregoing.
In this regard we cannot help quoting Sir Richard
Burton whose words are most apt: "The reader will
remember that the Hindus, as a rule, are a race of
vegetarians, who rarely drink any stimulant such as
wine, ale and spirits, or even tea, coffee and choco-
late. They look with horror upon the meat-eater,
who makes his body a grave for the corpses of animals; and they attach a bad name to all narcotics
except tobacco, leaving opium and hashish to low
fellows and ribald debauchees. It is evident that
under such circumstances, their desires, after the
first heat of youth, will be comparatively cold, and
that both sexes, especially the weaker, require to be
excited by a multitude and a variety of preliminaries
to possession, which would defeat their own object
in the case of Europeans. Thus we may account for
their faith in pepper, ginger, cloves, cinnamon, and
other spices which go by the name of *garm masálá*,
or hot condiments; these would have scanty effect
upon the beef-eating and beer-imbibing Briton, but
they exert a sufficiently powerful action upon a people comprised entirely of water-drinkers and rice
or pulse-feeders."

Preliminaries to Possession

Hence the extreme importance placed upon the external enjoyments, the caress and all its forms; embraces, kisses, unguiculations, morsitations, manipulations of the hair, patting, sighing, and other amorous blandishments too numerous to mention; in fact, all the processes which the Hindus believe should precede congress. "These affect the senses and divert the mind from coyness and coldness. After which tricks and toyings, the lover will proceed to complete possession," wisely counsels the sage.

But it must not be concluded that the Hindu follows slavishly the dictates of his master eroticians. On the contrary, they counsel the exercise of the individual's judgment whenever general rules appear inadequate or inappropriate. Burton notes a valid exception in the seventh great province of the caress as indicated by these eroticians. "Men who are well acquainted with the art of love are well aware how often one woman differs from another in her sighs and sounds during the time of congress. Some women like to be talked to in the most loving way, others in the most abusive way, and so on. Some women enjoy themselves with closed eyes in silence, others make a great noise over it, and some almost faint away. The great art is to ascertain what gives them the greatest pleasure, and what specialties they like best."

Vatsya Yana expresses this attitude in words that sum up the Hindu view and which are representative of the majority of sages and erotic guides:

"Such passionate actions and amorous gesticulations or movements, which arise on the spur of the moment, cannot be defined, and are as irregular as dreams. A horse having once attained the fifth degree of motion goes on with blind speed, regardless of pits, ditches, and posts in his way; and in the same manner a loving pair become blind in the heat of passion, and continue with great impetuosity paying not the least regard to excess. For this reason one who is well acquainted with the Science of Love, and knowing his own strength as also the tenderness, impetuosity, and strength of the young woman, should act accordingly. The various preliminaries to possession are not for all times or for all persons, but they should only be used at the proper time, and in the proper countries and places."

The true purpose of these classifications is hereby adumbrated. These steps and groupings are intended as a propadeutic to the Science of Love. The entire field of physical love is unfolded before the student; he weighs all the possible combinations and chooses for the enhancement of the woman's pleasure, her peculiar sensitivity and temperament. Moreover, by means of symbols a couple may make known to each other their desires without the knowledge of other persons. The brunt of the work is naturally placed on the shoulders of the man; the coyness of the woman is in some degree removed so that she becomes a willing partner to the tasks of love. Finally, the possibilities of love are exploited to their utmost degree, thus insuring a maximum both of the intensity and duration of sexual passion among a people to whom love is wholly sensual without a trace of that spiritual quality which informs and pervades the love-relations of our own civilization.

VII
The 243 Modes of Congress

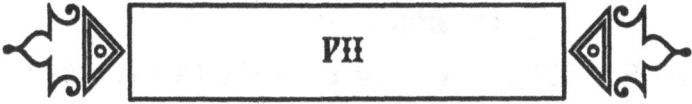

THE
TWO
HUNDRED
FORTY
THREE
MODES
OF
CONGRESS

Judged by the classics and classical eroticists of
India, the culminating province of the Hindu Art
of Love is sexual congress. Climate and custom and
the weary weight of centuries all conspire to shape
the Hindu into the amorous creature that he is. Even

the Sacred Laws of Manu, as we shall afterwards observe, are twisted into tricky technicalities to encour-
age a host of shameless liberties between the sexes.
We do not wish to obtrude our personal views here
which would clearly indicate how this amorousness
of the Hindu has destroyed his character and health
and has led to a racial and national stagnation which
is one of the sore spots of oriental civilization. Suffice
it to point out in this place that not only is sexual
congress the perpetual subject of discussion among
Hindus but that they justify this preoccupation with
sex by maintaining that it is the subject most worthy
of discussion and investigation.

The Hindu eroticists characteristically disregard
the necessity for a description of the male organ of
generation, the lingam, and devote their serious attention to a study of the female organ.

Their anatomical description of the yoni is naturally very inexact from a physiological standpoint.
The more ancient *Kama Sutra* is silent on this score
and the more modern *Ananga Ranga* gives the following description: "In the yoni there is an artery
called saspanda which corresponds with that of the
lingam, and which, when excited, causes kama-salila
to flow. It is inside and towards the navel, and it is
attached to certain roughnesses, which are peculiarly

liable to induce the paroxysm when subjected to friction. The madana-chatra (clitoris), in the upper part of the yoni, is that portion which projects like the plantain-shoot sprouting from the ground; it is connected with the mada-vahi (sperm-flowing) artery, and causes the latter to overflow. Finally, there is an artery, termed purna-chandra, which is full of the kama-salila, and to this the learned men of old attribute the monthly ailment." It need hardly be remarked that the Hindus believed the kama-salila of women to be in every way like that of men; the modern microscope was necessary before we discovered that the spermatozoid was an attribute of the male sex only.

Kinds of Congress according to Dimensions: The reader will recall the division of man into three classes (hare-man, bull-man, and horse-man) according to the size of his lingam, and that woman was also divided into three classes (deer-woman, mare-woman, and elephant-woman) according to the depth of her yoni.

There are consequently nine combinations: three unions of equal kind between persons of corresponding dimensions; and six unions of unequal kind between persons of varying dimensions. The equal unions are the hare with the deer, the bull with the mare, and the horse with the elephant. The unequal unions are the hare with the mare or elephant, the bull with the deer or elephant and the horse with the deer or mare.

The horse and mare, or the bull and deer, form the high alliances; the horse and deer form the highest. The elephant and bull, or the mare and hare, form low alliances; the elephant and hare form the lowest. The equal unions are considered the best; the highest and lowest unions are the worst; the rest are middling, the high being better than the low.

Kinds of Congress according to Force of Passion: Each of these nine combinations is subdivided into nine other classes. The first three are related to force of passion or the capacity for enjoyment: of these, the furious appetite is the highest capacity; next is the moderate desire; then the slow or cold concupiscence which is the lowest capacity for enjoyment.

Kinds of Congress according to Duration of Passion: The next three concern the duration of the preliminary caresses: first, those efforts which continue for a long time before they bring on the climax; second, those which extend for a moderate time; and finally, the shortest.

The 243 Modes of Congress

Kinds of Congress according to Frequency of Passion: The last three cover the forms of emission of the kama-salila, according to the length or shortness of time: that which occupies a great length of time; that which is accomplished within a moderate period; and that which takes only a short time to finish.

On this matter, Kalyana Malla makes a mathematical observation: "Thus we may observe that there are nine separate forms of congress according to the length and depth of the organs. There are also nine, determined by the longer or shorter period required to induce the climax, and there are nine which arise from the preparations which lead to the conclusion. Altogether we have twenty-seven distinct kinds of congress which, by multiplying the nine species and the three periods give *a grand total of two hundred and forty-three.*"

There are certain places where women are not to be enjoyed under any conditions: the place where fire is lighted by religious formulæ; in the presence of a Brahman or any other religious man; under the eyes of an aged person to whom respect is due; when a great man is looking on; by the side of a river or any murmuring stream; at a place for drawing water; in a temple dedicated to the gods; in a fort or castle; in a prison; on a highway; in the house of another person; in the forest; in a meadow or other open place; and in a graveyard. The consequences of carnal connection at such places are held to be disastrous; they always breed misfortunes and if any children result they become malicious persons.

There are also certain times when women are not to be enjoyed: by day, unless their class and temperament require coition during the light hours; when the sun or a planet passes from one side of the zodiac to another; during the cold season (October to November); during the hot season (June to July); the new-moon day of the month except in cases where the *Kama Shastra* specifies to the contrary; during the periods when the man's body suffers from fever; during religious duties; in the evening time, and when wearied with warfare. The same disastrous results as above apply to these prohibitions of congress.

In addition to restrictions of place and time, there are also certain conditions when women are not to be enjoyed: a pregnant woman; one who has not long left the lying-in chamber; a woman suffering from fever or other weakening complaint; a girl not yet arrived at puberty, etc. The list of such qualifying conditions is too long to deserve further itemization.

The 243 Modes of Congress

The following women are not to be enjoyed under any circumstances; a leper; a lunatic; a woman turned out of caste; a woman who reveals secrets; a woman who publicly expresses a desire for intercourse; a woman who is extremely white; a woman who is extremely black; a foul-smelling woman; a woman who is a near-relation; a woman who is a female friend; a woman who leads the life of an ascetic; and the wife of a relation, of a friend, of a learned Brahman, and of the King. But there is an amusing codicil to these exceptions: If any of the above women has been enjoyed by five men, she is a fit and proper person to be enjoyed! Such are the hypocritical subterfuges of the Hindu erotologists!

There are detailed instructions for the place best fitted for congress: Choose the largest, and finest, and the most airy room in the house, purify it thoroughly with whitewash, and decorate its spacious and beautiful walls with pictures and other objects upon which the eye may dwell with delight. Scattered about this room should be musical instruments, especially the pipe and the lute; with refreshments, as cocoanut, betel-leaf and milk, which is so useful for retaining and restoring vigor; bottles of rose water and various essences, fans and chauris for cooling the air, and books containing amorous songs, tales and descriptions, and gladdening the glance with illustrations of love-postures. Splendid wall-lights should gleam around the hall, reflected by a hundred mirrors, whilst both man and woman should contend against any reserve or false shame, giving themselves up in complete nudity to unrestrained voluptuousness, upon a high and handsome bedstead, raised on tall legs, furnished with many pillows, and covered by a rich canopy; the sheets being besprinkled with flowers and the coverlets scented by burning luscious incense, such as aloes and other fragrant woods.

In such a place the nayaka should receive the woman, who will come bathed and dressed, and invite her to take refreshment and to drink freely. He should then seat her on his left side, and, holding her hair and touching also the end and knot of her garment, he should gently embrace her with his right arm. They should then carry on an amusing conversation on various subjects, and may also talk suggestively of things which might be considered as coarse, or not to be mentioned generally in society. They may then sing, either with or without gesticulations, and play on musical instruments, talk about the arts, and persuade each other to drink. At last, when the woman is overcome with love and desire, the lover should proceed with all the preliminaries to possession as taught by the masters.

At the end of the congress, the lovers, with modesty, and not looking at each other, should go separately to the wash-room. After this, sitting in their own places, they should eat some betel-leaves, and the lover should apply to the body of the woman some pleasant sandalwood ointment, or ointment of some other kind. He should then embrace her with his left arm, and with agreeable words should give her water to drink. They can then eat sweetmeats, or anything else, according to their liking, and may drink fresh juice, soup, gruel, extracts of meat, sherbet, the juice of mango fruits, citron juice mixed with sugar, or anything relished in different countries and known to be sweet, soft, and pure. The lovers may also sit on the terrace of the palace or house, and enjoy the moonlight, and carry on an agreeable conversation. At this time, too, while the woman lies in his lap, with her face towards the moon, the lover should show her the different planets, the morning star, the polar star, and the Great Bear.

Before proceeding to the various modes of congress, there are certain signs by which the learned Hindus ascertain that the paroxysm in women has

taken place. These signs will be obvious to every
married man and therefore require no elaboration
here. But the eroticists do not content themselves
with the outward and obvious. They find meaning
in the condition of the woman's eyes, the accelera-
tion of her breathing, the muscular movement of
her limbs, and an endless variety of other tokens.

At this point we may be permitted to quote the
apt words of Kalyana Malla: "The chief reason for
the separation of the married couple and the cause
which drives the husband to the embrace of strange
women, and the wife to the arms of strange men, is
the want of varied pleasures and the monotony which
follows possession. There is no doubt about it. Monotony begets satiety, and satiety distaste for congress, especially in one or the other; malicious feelings are engendered, the husband or the wife yields
to temptation, and the other follows, being driven
by jealousy. . . . Fully understanding the way in
which such quarrels arise, I have shown how the husband, by varying the enjoyment of his wife, may live
with her as with thirty-two different women, ever
varying the enjoyment of her, and rendering satiety
impossible."

Due to moral and legal reasons we are unable,
even in such a work as the present, intended solely

The 243 Modes of Congress

for adult students of anthropology and comparative ethnology, to follow Kalyana Malla and other Hindu sages into their intimate pedagogics. For the immemorial guidance of these teachers derives from certain high mysteries of eroticism conditioned chiefly upon the exceeding pliability of the Hindu's limbs. This enables him to assume attitudes absolutely impossible to others. Many of the postures seem almost indistinguishable without the aid of diagrams and extensive descriptions. Moreover, the height and recessiveness of the parts of Hindu women are such as conduce to a more intricate art of love than is anatomically possible to any other Oriental or Occidental race.

Because of these reasons we must content ourselves with but a rough, fragmentary classification of the main postures. We deeply regret that necessity of clothing this aspect of Hindu love in none too clear a light and in none too detailed a manner, and accordingly render our due apologies to the reader.

There are five great divisions of congress:

1. *Standing*
2. *Supine*
3. *Sitting*
4. *Lying*
5. *Prone*

The Hindu Art of Love

In the first division there are eleven categories

1. *The Rustling of the Dove's Nest*
2. *The Beating about the Bushes*
3. *The Retro-circle*
4. *The Bending of the Rainbow*
5. *The Embrace of the Reindeers*
6. *The Blow of the Anvil*
7. *The Breath of the Dragon*
8. *The Form of the Bow*
9. *The Leap of the Goat*
10. *The Flight of the Arrow*
11. *The Union of the Souls*

In the second division there are three categories

1. *The Crossing of the Bridge*
2. *The Bending of the Pines*
3. *The Backward Flight of the Eagle*

In the third division there are ten categories:

1. *The Stitch of the Tailor*
2. *The Lift of the Warrior*
3. *Splitting of the Mango*
4. *The Cradle Posture*
5. *The Raising of the Palm*
6. *The Tortoise Posture*
7. *The Triple Tortoise Posture*

The 243 Modes of Congress

8. *The Wish-Bone Posture*
9. *The Striking of the Clock*
10. *The Turning of the Wheel*

In the fourth division there are three categories:

1. *The Pillowing of the Knees*
2. *The Stork Stance*
3. *The Lift of the Devil*

In the fifth division there are two categories:

1. *The Cow Posture*
2. *The Elephant Posture*

There are further provinces of congress which demonstrate beyond cavil the immoral absorption of the Hindu with sensual behavior. An illuminating commentary however of his sensuality is that his extravagant lewdness does not include any of the sexual perversions between men and men, or women with women, with the rarest of exceptions despite the prevalence of harems and polygamy.

VIII
Courtship and Marriage

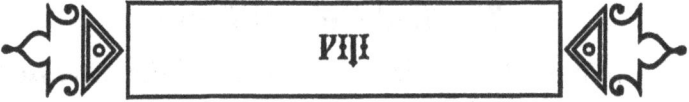

COURTSHIP
AND
MARRIAGE

In India, where woman is more loved than courted, and more courted than married, it is natural for the social organism to place the greatest importance on marriage. It becomes the sacred duty of man and woman and the most important obligation of parents. The latter enjoy few of the promised blessings if their daughter is unmarried and childless, and to the girl herself, marriage is the supreme sacrament.

It should be stated at this point that polygamy is not only tolerated and sanctioned in India but that the *Laws of Manu* expressly stipulate that men may marry as many wives, and by custom maintain as many concubines, as they choose. The reader should bear this condition in mind as well as the system of child marriages, for these customs underpin the foundation of Hindu courtship.

A comprehensive picture of the complexities and strict laws in connection with marriage and the caste system universal in India is afforded by the Sacred Books of Manu. We shall pass over these sacred writings, however, as too involved for American readers and borrow instead from the classic eroticists who are nearer the heart, so to speak, of Hindu courtship and marriage.

The numerous pictures of courtship and marriage presented by these sages delineate perfectly the erotic social habits of the Hindus. The general impression of this dazzling panorama of Hindu love-life seems a bizarre amalgam of sacred and profane love. The eroticists begin with the fundamental axiom that when a girl of the same caste, and a virgin, is married to a man in accordance with the precepts of Holy Writ, the results of the union are: the acquisition of Dharma and Artha, offspring, affinity, increase of friends and untarnished love. Of course, they prescribe strict rules for a girl taken as wife: She should come from a family of equal rank with that of her husband, a house which is known to be valiant and chaste, wise and learned, prudent and patient, correct and becomingly behaved, and famed for acting according to its religion, and for discharging its social duties. She should be free from vices, and endowed with all good qualities, possess a fair face and a fine person, have brothers and kinsfolk, and be very proficient in the Art of Love.

Beauty and fair shape of body are highly desirable and reside in the maiden whose face is soft and pleasing as the moon; whose eyes are bright and liquid as the faun's; whose nose is delicate as the sesamum flowers; whose teeth are clean as diamonds and clear as pearls; whose ears are small and rounded; whose neck is like a sea-shell, with three delicate lines or tracings behind; whose lower lip is red as the ripe fruit of the bryony; whose hair is black as the black-bee's wing; whose skin is brilliant as the flower of the dark-blue lotus, or light as the surface of polished gold; whose feet and hands are red, being marked with the circular discus; whose stomach is small, the umbilical region being drawn in; whose shape below the hips is large; whose thighs, being well-proportioned and pleasing as the plantain tree, make her walk like the elephant, neither too fast nor too slow; and whose voice is sweet as the Kokila bird's. Such a girl, especially if her temper be good, her nature kindly, her sleep short, and her mind and body not inclined to laziness, should at once be married to the wise man.

Now in order to bring about a marriage with a girl as above described, the parents and relations of the man should exert themselves, and also such friends on both sides as may be required to assist in the matter. These friends should bring to the notice of the girl's parents, the faults, both present and future, of all the other men who may wish to marry her. At the same time they should extol even to exaggeration all the excellences, ancestral and paternal, of their friend, so as to endear him to them, and particularly to those that may be liked by the girl's mother. One of the friends should also disguise himself as an astrologer, and declare the future good fortune and wealth of his friend by showing the

existence of all the lucky omens, the good influence
of planets, the auspicious entrance of the sun into a
sign of the Zodiac, and propitious and fortunate
marks on his body. Others again should rouse the
jealousy of the girl's mother by telling her that their
friend has a chance of getting from some other quarter even a better girl than hers.

A girl should be taken as a wife, and also given
in marriage, when fortune, signs, omens and the
words of others are favorable for, according to
Ghotakamukha, a man should not marry at any
time he chooses.

The following are the girls to be carefully avoided
under all circumstances: The girl who comes from
a bad family; whose body is either very short or
very tall, very fat or very thin; whose skin is ever
rough and hard; whose hair and eyes are yellowish
and like a cat's; whose teeth are long, or are wholly
wanting; whose mouth and lips are wide and project-
ing, with the lower lip of dark color, and tremulous
when speaking; who allows her tongue to loll out;
whose eyebrows are straight; whose temples are de-
pressed; who shows signs of beard, mustaches, and
much body-hair; whose neck is thick; who has some
limbs shorter and others longer than the usual proportion; whose one breast is large or high, and the

other small or low; whose ears are triangular, like a sifting or winnowing fan; whose second toe is larger and longer than the big toe; whose third toe is blunt, without tip or point, and whose little toes do not touch the ground; whose voice is harsh and laughter loud; who walks quickly and with uncertain gait; who is full-grown; who is disposed to be sickly, and who bears the name of a mountain, of a tree, of a river, of a bird, or of a constellation. Such a girl, especially if her disposition be irascible and temper violent; if she eats and sleeps much; if she is always vexed, troubled and distressed; if her disposition is restless and fidgety; if she has little understanding in worldly matters; if she is destitute of shame and if her natural disposition is wicked— such a girl should by all means be avoided by the wise man.

The man should also be tried, even as gold is tested, in four ways: by the touchstone, by cutting, by heating, and by hammering. Thus there must be taken into consideration: learning, disposition, qualities, and action. The first characteristic of a man is courage, with endurance; if he attempt any deed, great or small, he should do it with the spirit of a lion. Second is prudence: time and place must be determined, and opportunity devised, like the heron that stands intently eyeing its prey in the pool below. The third is early rising, and causing others to do the same. The fourth is hardihood in war. The fifth is a generous distribution of food and property among family and friends. The sixth is duly attending to the wants of the wife. The seventh is circumspection in love matters. The eighth is secrecy and privacy in the venereal act. The ninth is patience and perseverance in all the business of life. The tenth is judgment in collecting and storing up what may be necessary. The eleventh is not to allow wealth and worldly success to engender pride and vanity, magnificence and ostentation. The twelfth is never aspiring to the unattainable. The thirteenth is contentment with what the man has, if he can get no more. The fourteenth is simplicity of diet. The fifteenth is the avoidance of over-sleep. The sixteenth is diligence in the service of employers. The seventeenth is not to fly when attacked by robbers and villains. The eighteenth is working willingly; for instance, not taking into consideration the sun and shade if the laborer be obliged to carry a parcel. The nineteenth is the patient endurance of trouble. The twentieth is the constant surveyance of a great business. And the twenty-first is reflection upon the means best suited for success. Any person who com-

bines these twenty-one qualities is deservedly re-
puted an excellent man, fit for marriage.

The father of the girl should look for the following characteristics in a prospective son-in-law: He
must come from a large family, which has never
known sin and poverty. He must be young, handsome, wealthy, brave and influential; diligent in
business, moderate in enjoying riches, sweet of
speech, well versed in discharging his own duties,
known to the world as a mine of virtues, steadfast in
mind, and a treasury of mercy, who gives alms and
makes charities as far as his means permit.

The father of the girl should also be careful that
none of the following defects and blemishes are
present in the suitor: The man who is born in a low
family, who is vicious, a libertine, pitiless, and ever
sickly with dangerous disease, sinful and very
wicked, poor and miserly, impotent, prone to conceal the virtues and to divulge the vices of others;
a constant traveller, an absentee, one ever away from
his home and residing abroad; a debtor, a beggar,
a man who has no friendship with the good, or who,
if he has it, breaks into quarrels upon trifling
matters.

When a girl becomes marriageable her parents
should dress her smartly, and should place her

where she can easily be seen by all. Every afternoon, having dressed her and decorated her in a becoming manner, they should send her with her female companions to sports, sacrifices, and marriage ceremonies, and thus show her to advantage in society, because she is a kind of merchandise.

They should also receive with kind words and signs of friendliness those men of an auspicious appearance who may come accompanied by their friends and relations for the purpose of marrying their daughter, and under some pretext or other, having first dressed her becomingly, should then present her to them. After this they should await the pleasure of fortune and with this object should appoint a future day on which an answer can be arranged with regard to their daughter's marriage. On this occasion when the persons have come, the parents of the girl should ask them to bathe and dine, and should say: "Everything will take place at the proper time." They should not then comply with the request, but should settle the matter later.

When a girl is thus acquired either according to the custom of the country, or according to his own desire, the man should marry her in conformity with the precepts of Holy Writ as described by Manu in his *Institutes of the Law.* There are in addition cer-

tain names given to mixed forms. A high connection
is when a man, after marrying a girl, has to serve
her and her relations afterwards like a servant. When
a man together with his relations lords it over his
wife, it is called a low connection. But when both the
man and the woman afford mutual pleasure to each
other, and where the relatives on both sides pay
respect to one another, it is called a proper connection. Therefore a man should contract neither a high
connection by which he is obliged to bow down afterwards to his kinsmen, nor a low connection, which
is universally reprehended by the wise.

One direct consequence of the Hindu system of
child marriage is the customary omission of cohabitation immediately after the wedding. Although
congress often takes place before the child-wife has
reached the age of puberty, it is considered a most
sacrilegious transgression if she menstruates, even
for the first time, before she has been enjoyed.

For the first three days after marriage, the girl
and her husband should sleep on the floor, abstain
from sexual pleasures, and eat their food without
seasoning it with alkali or salt. For the next seven
days they should bathe amidst the sounds of auspicious musical instruments, should decorate themselves, dine together, and pay attention to their rela-

tions as well as to those who may have come to witness their marriage. This is applicable to persons of all castes. On the night of the tenth day the man should begin in a lonely place with soft words, and thus create confidence in the girl. Some authors say that for the purpose of conquering her he should not speak to her for three days, but the followers of Babhravya are of the opinion that if the man does not speak to her for three days, the girl may be discouraged by seeing him spiritless like a pillar, and, becoming dejected, she may begin to despise him as a eunuch.

Vatsya Yana says that the man should begin to win her over, and to create confidence in her, but should abstain at first from sexual pleasures. Women being of a tender nature want tender beginnings, and when they are forcibly approached by men with whom they are but slightly acquainted, they sometimes suddenly become haters of sexual connection, and sometimes even haters of the male sex. The man should therefore approach the girl according to her liking, and should make use of those devices by which he may be able to establish himself more and more into her confidence.

The following are the main methods: He should embrace her with the upper part of his body, because that is easier and simpler. If the girl is grown up, or if the man has known her for some time, he may embrace her by the light of a lamp, but if he is not well acquainted with her, or if she is a young girl, he should embrace her in darkness.

When the girl accepts the embrace, the man should put a tambula, a chew of betel nut and betel leaves, in her mouth. If she refuses to take it he should induce her to do so by conciliatory words, entreaties, oaths and kneelings at her feet, for it is a universal rule that however angry or bashful a woman may be, she never disregards a man's kneeling at her feet. At the time of giving this tambula, he should kiss her mouth softly and gracefully without making any sound. When she is gained over in this respect he should then induce her to talk by asking questions about things of which he knows or pretends to know nothing, and which can be answered in a few words. If she does not speak to him he should not frighten her, but should repeat the same questions again and again in a conciliatory manner.

If she does not then speak he should urge her to reply because, as Ghotakamukha says, "All girls hear everything said to them by men, but sometimes do not themselves say a single word." When she is thus importuned, the girl should give replies by shakes of the head, but if she has quarrelled with the man she should not even do that. When she is asked by the man whether she prays for him and whether she likes him she should remain silent for a long time, and when at last importuned to reply, should give him a favorable answer by a nod of her head.

If the girl is familiar with the man, she should place near him, without saying anything, the tambula, the ointment, or the garland that he may have asked for, or she may tie them up in his upper garment. While she is engaged in this, the man should touch her young breasts by pressing with the nails, and if she prevents him from doing this, he should say to her, "I will not do so again if you will embrace me," and should in this way cause her to embrace him.

While he is being embraced by her he should pass his hand repeatedly over her body. By and by he should place her in his lap, and try more and more to gain her consent, and if she will not yield to him he should frighten her by saying, "I shall impress marks of my teeth and nails on your lips and breasts, and then make similar marks on my own body, and shall tell my friends that you made them. What will you say then?" In this and other ways, as fear and confidence are created in the minds of children, so should the man win his child-wife to his wishes.

On the second and third nights, after her confidence has increased still more, he should feel the whole of her body with his hands, and kiss her lovingly; he should also place his hands upon her neck and if she permits this he should then stroke the joints of her limbs. If she tries to prevent him from doing this he should say to her, "What harm is there in doing it?" and should persuade her to let him do it. After gaining this point he should touch her, loosen her girdle and the knot of her dress, and turning up her lower garment should stroke her naked knees.

Under various pretences he should do all these things, but he should not at that time begin actual congress. After this he should teach her the sixty-four arts of love, should tell her how much he loves her, and describe to her the hopes which he formerly entertained regarding her. He should also promise to be faithful to her in the future, and should dispel all her fears with respect to rivals, and, at last, after having overcome her bashfulness, he should begin to enjoy her in a way that does not frighten her.

In general, a man acting according to the inclinations of a girl should try to win her so that she may love him and place her confidence in him. A man does not succeed either by implicitly following the inclination of a girl, or by wholly opposing her, and he should therefore adopt a middle course. He who knows how to make himself beloved by women, as well as to increase their honor and create confidence in them, such a man becomes an object of their love. But he, who neglects a girl thinking that she is too bashful, is despised by her as a beast ignorant of the workings of the female mind.

Moreover, a child-wife forced by one who does not understand the hearts of girls becomes nervous, uneasy, and dejected, and suddenly begins to hate the man who has taken advantage of her; she then sinks into despondency, and becomes either a hater of mankind altogether or, hating her own husband, has recourse to other men.

For certain classes of men there are different methods of courtship. A poor man of good qualities, a man born of a low family and possessing mediocre qualities, a neighbor of wealth, and one under the control of his father, mother or brothers, should not marry without endeavoring to win a girl from her childhood so that she may love and esteem him. Thus a young man separated from his parents, and living in the house of his uncle, should try to win the daughter of his uncle, or some other girl even though she be previously betrothed to another. Ghotakamukha says that this way of winning a girl is unexceptionable because Dharma can be accomplished by means of it, as well as by any other forms of marriage.

When a young man has thus begun to woo the girl he loves, he should spend his time with her and amuse her with various games and diversions fitted for their age and acquaintanceship, such as picking and collecting flowers, making garlands of flowers, playing the parts of members of a fictitious family, cooking food, playing with dice, playing with cards, the game of odd and even, the game of finding out the middle finger, the game of six pebbles, and such other games as may be prevalent in the country and agreeable to the disposition of the girl. In addition to this he should carry on various amusing games, played by several persons together, such as hide and seek, playing with seeds, hiding things in several small heaps of wheat and looking for them, blindman's bluff, gymnastic exercises, and other games of the same sort in company with the girl, her friends and female attendants.

The man should also manifest great kindness to any woman whom the girl thinks fit to be trusted, and should also make new acquaintances. But above all, he should attach to himself by kindness and little services the daughter of the girl's nurse, for if she be won over to his side, she will not only not obstruct his design but is sometimes even able to effect an union between him and the girl. Moreover, she will always talk of his many excellent qualities to the parents and relations of the girl.

In this way the man should do whatever the girl takes most delight in, and he should get for her whatever she may desire to own. Thus he should procure for her such playthings as may be hardly known to other girls. He may also show her a ball dyed with various colors, and other curiosities of the same sort; he should give her dolls made of cloth, wood, buffalo-horn, ivory, wax, flour or earth; also utensils for cooking food, and figures in wood, such as a man and woman standing, a pair of rams, or goats, or sheep; also temples made of earth, bamboo or wood, dedicated to various goddesses; and cages for parrots, cuckoos, starlings, quails, cocks, and partridges; water vessels of different sorts and of elegant forms, machines for throwing water about, guitars, stands for images, stools, red arsenic, yellow ointment, vermilion and collyrium, as well as sandalwood, saffron, betel nuts and betel leaves. Such things should be given at different times whenever he gets a good opportunity of meeting her, some being given in private, and some in public, according to circumstances. In short, he should try in every way to make her look upon him as one who would obey all her wishes.

In the next place, he should get her to meet him privately in some place, and should then tell her that the reason of his secretly giving her presents was the fear that the parents of both of them might be displeased, and then he may add that the things which he has given her are very much desired by other people. When her love begins to show signs of increasing he should relate to her agreeable stories if she expresses a wish to hear such narratives. Or if she takes delight in legerdemain, he should amaze her by performing various tricks of jugglery. Or if she is curious to see a performance of the various arts, he should show his own skill in them. When she is delighted with singing he should entertain her with music, and on certain days and at moonlight fairs and festivals, he should present her with bouquets of flowers, with chaplets for the head and with ear ornaments and rings.

He should also teach the daughter of the girl's nurse all the sixty-four means of pleasure practised by men, and under this pretext should also inform her of his great skill in the art of sexual enjoyment. All this time he should wear fine clothes and make as presentable an appearance as possible, for young women want the men who live with them to look handsome and well dressed.

Now a girl always shows her love by outward signs and actions such as the following: She never looks the man in the face, and becomes abashed when she is looked at by him; under some pretext or other she shows her limbs to him; she looks secretly at him though he has gone away from her side; hangs down her head when asked some question by him, and answers in indistinct words and unfinished sentences; delights to be in his company for a long time, speaks to her attendants in a peculiar tone with the hope of attracting his attention towards her when she is at a distance from him; does not wish to leave the place where he is; under some pretext or other she makes him look at different objects; narrates to him tales and stories very slowly, so that she may continue conversing with him for a long time; kisses and embraces before him a child sitting in her lap; draws ornamental marks on the foreheads of her female servants; performs sportive and graceful movements when her attendants speak jestingly to her in the presence of her lover; confides in her

lover's friends, and respects and obeys them; shows
kindness to his servants, converses with them, and
engages them to do her work as if she were their
mistress; listens attentively to them when they tell
stories about her lover to someone else; enters his
house when induced to do so by the daughter of her
nurse, and by her assistance manages to converse
and play with him; avoids being seen by her lover
when she is not dressed or decorated; presents him
through her female friend her ear ornament, ring,
or garland of flowers that he may have asked to see;
always wears anything that he may have presented
to her; becomes dejected when any other bridegroom
is mentioned by her parents; and does not mix with
those who may be of his party or who may support
his claims.

Now when the girl begins to show her love by outward signs and motions, as have just been described,
the lover should try to win her completely by various
means, such as the following: When engaged with
her in any game or sport he should intentionally
hold her hand. He should try to practise the various kinds of caresses, as described in the chapter
on the *Preliminaries to Possession*. He should show
her the images of human beings cut out of the leaves
of a tree. When engaged in water sports, he should

dive at a distance from her, and come up close to her. He should show an increased liking for the new foliage of trees. He should describe to her the pangs he suffers on her account. He should relate to her the beautiful dream that he has had with reference to other women. At parties and assemblies of his caste he should sit near her, and touch her under some pretence or other, and having placed his foot upon hers, he should slowly touch each of her toes, and press the ends of the nails; if successful in this, he should take hold of her foot with his hand and repeat the same thing. When he gives anything to her or takes anything from her, he should show her by his manner and looks how much he loves her. He should sprinkle upon her the water brought for rinsing his mouth. When alone with her in a lonely place, or in darkness, he should make love to her, and tell her the true state of his mind without distressing her in any way.

Whenever he sits with her on the same seat or bed he should say to her, "I have something to tell you in private," and then, when she comes to hear it in a quiet place, he should express his love to her more by manner and signs than by words. When he comes to know the state of her feelings towards him he should pretend to be ill, and should make her come

The Hindu Art of Love

to his house to visit him. There he should intentionally hold her hand and place it on his eyes and
forehead and ask her to prepare some medicine for
him in the following words: "This work must be
done by you, and by no one else."

When she wants to leave he should allow her to
go with an earnest request to come and see him
again. This pretence at illness should be continued
for three days and nights. Afterwards, when she
comes to see him frequently, he should carry on long
conversations with her for, according to Ghotakamukha, "though a man loves a girl ever so much, he
never succeeds in winning her without a great deal
of talking." At last, when the man finds the girl
ready to submit, he may begin to enjoy her.

When it is impossible for the man to carry on his
endeavors alone, he should, by means of the daughter of her nurse, or a female friend in whom she confides, arrange to meet the girl without making known
to her his design, and he should then proceed with
her in the manner above described. Or he should in
the beginning send his own female servant to live
with the girl as her friend, and should then conquer
her accordingly.

At last when he knows the state of her feelings by
her outward manner and conduct towards him at

religious ceremonies, marriage ceremonies, fairs, festivals, theatres, public assemblies, and suchlike occasions, he should begin to enjoy her when she is alone, for Vatsya Yana lays down the universal rule that women, when resorted to at proper times and in proper places, do not turn away from their lovers.

When a girl, possessed of good qualities and well-bred, though born in a humble family, or destitute of wealth and therefore not desired by her equals, or an orphan girl, or one deprived of her parents but observing the rules of her family and caste, should wish to bring about her own marriage when she comes of age, such a girl should endeavor to tempt a strong and good looking young man, or a person whom she thinks would marry her on account of the weakness of his mind, and even without the consent of his parents.

She should do this by such means as would endear her to this person, as well as by frequently seeing and meeting him. Her mother should also constantly cause them to meet by means of her female friends, and the daughter of her nurse. The girl herself should try to be alone with her beloved in some quiet place, and at odd times should give him flowers, betel nuts, betel leaves, and perfumes. She should also show her skill in the practise of the arts, in shampooing, in scratching, and in pressing with the nails. She should also talk to him on the subjects he likes best, and discuss with him the ways and means of winning the affections of a girl.

But according to the ancient eroticists even though the girl loves the man ever so much, she should not offer herself, or make the first overtures, for a girl who does this loses her dignity, and is liable to be scorned and rejected. But when the man shows his wish to enjoy her, she should be favorable to him and should show no change in her demeanor when he embraces her, and should receive all the manifestations of his love as if she were ignorant of the state of his mind. But when he tries to kiss her she should oppose him; and when he attempts to have sexual intercourse with her she should let him touch her intimately only with considerable difficulty; and though importuned, she should not yield herself up to him as if of her own accord, but should resist his attempts to possess her. Moreover, it is only when she is certain that she is truly loved, and that her lover is indeed devoted to her and will not quickly change his affections, that she should give herself to him completely and then persuade him to marry her quickly. Curiously enough, many eroticists including Vatsya Yana command that a girl tell all her friends as soon as she has lost her virginity!

In the above cases there are set aside different forms of marriage from those enumerated by Manu and which must be strictly followed. When the girl is seduced, and acts openly with the man as his wife, he should cause fire to be brought from the house of a Brahman, and having spread the Kusha grass upon the ground and offered an oblation to the fire, he should marry her according to the precepts of religion. After this he must inform his parents of the facts, because according to the ancient law-givers, a marriage solemnly contracted in the presence of fire cannot afterwards be set aside.

After the consummation of the marriage, the relatives of the man should gradually be made acquainted with the affair, and the relations of the girl should also be apprised of it in such a way that they may consent to the marriage, and overlook the manner in which it was brought about. When this is done they should afterwards be reconciled by affectionate presents and favorable conduct. This manner is called the Gandharva form of marriage.

If the girl cannot make up her mind, or will not express her readiness to marry, the man may trick her, say the sages, in one of the following ways:

On a fitting occasion and under some excuse, he should, by means of a female friend with whom he is well acquainted and whom he can trust and who also is well known to the girl's family, have the girl brought unexpectedly to his house. Whereupon, he should bring fire from the house of a Brahman and proceed as above.

When the marriage of the girl to some other person draws near the man should disparage the future husband to the girl's mother, and then having got the girl to come with her mother's consent to a neighboring house, he should bring fire from the house of a Brahman, and proceed as above.

The man should become a great friend of the brother of the girl, and if the brother is about his own age and addicted to prostitutes and to intrigues with other men's wives, he should give him assistance in such matters and also occasional gifts. He should then tell him about his great love for his sister, as young men will sacrifice even their lives for the sake of those who may be of the same age, habits and dispositions as themselves. After this the man should have the girl brought by means of her brother to some secure place and, having brought fire from the house of a Brahman, proceed as above.

The man should on the occasion of festivals get

the daughter of the girl's nurse to give the girl some intoxicating drink, and then cause her to be brought to some secure place under the pretence of some business, and there, having seduced her before she recovers from her intoxication, should bring fire from the house of a Brahman and proceed as above.

The man should, with the connivance of the daughter of the nurse, carry off the girl from her house while she is asleep and then, having enjoyed her before she recovers from her sleep, should bring fire from the house of a Brahman and proceed as above.

When the girl goes to a garden or to some village in the neighborhood, the man should with his friends fall on her guards and, having killed them or frightened them away and forcibly carried her off, should take her virginity, and then proceed as above.

These forms of marriage are here enumerated in the order of their merit and in accordance with the commands of religion. Only when it is impossible to carry out the first method should the second method of effecting marriage be resorted to, and so on in the above sequence.

IX

The Ganika or Glorified Prostitution

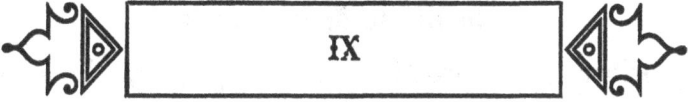

THE
GANIKA
OR
GLORIFIED
PROSTITUTION

Unequalled in any country or literature is the Hindu's high respect and unbounded admiration for the prostitute who is expert in all the ways of love and congress. She is called *ganika* and her traditional position in India is nothing less than a glorification of prostitution. The ganika, who is a prostitute by choice and love, irresistibly reminds the student of comparative ethnology of the hetæræ of ancient Greece and the geisha of the Japanese.

To honor such a profession is almost unthinkable to the American sense of values and nothing short of a long residence in India can alter such deep-rooted prejudice. Yet the entire background of the Hindu Art of Love is colored by the ganika and her position and influence in society. Her name literally signifies a woman who is a member of a gana or corporation and whose charms are the common property and pleasure of men.

Manu associates the gana and the ganika in one passage saying that the food offered by both is equally to be refused by a Brahman. The gana may be a corporation of citizens, such as the gatherings of the nayaka, or it may be a political body like that of the ancient Licchains of Vaisali.

We read in the Mahavagga that Ambapolika, the ganika of Vaisali, was charming, attractive, graceful, generous, and proficient in song, dance and music. The wealth and power that she possessed and the position she occupied were in no way inferior to those of the richest Licchains; her train was as numerous and as sumptuously decorated, her carriages as magnificent as those of the haughty Licchains against whom she drove up, axle to axle, wheel to wheel, and yoke to yoke. Her presence made the city of Vaisali shine forth in dazzling splendor. She constituted the most valued institution of the city. The high model of beauty and art thus set up by the ganika of Vaisali roused a merchant of the rival city of Rajagaha to induce King Bimbisara to establish ganikas in his own capital.

From Bharata we learn that in those ancient days ganikas were not as numerous as they became in the time of Vatsya Yana. It was principally in the days of Katya Yana, the author of the Varttika Sutras of the rhetorical school of Panini, that the Hindus had taken them to their hearts and established guilds of ganikas (ganikyam), as is explained in the Mahabhashya.

We may also observe the significant fact that Buddha excludes from his chosen fold the eunuch and the hermaphrodite, but not the ganika. The Buddhist religious books have hardly anything to say against Ambapolika, nor do they intimate anything peculiar or out of the way in the favor shown her by Buddha. Reading the Vinaya Pittaka we are indeed astonished to learn how careful and anxious Buddha was not to offend public opinion and to give an appearance of decency to his chosen congregation. Although he thought it disreputable to the public decency to harbor sinners like the parricide or the matricide, he manifested no difficulty in regularly ordaining a prostitute.

This attitude is further evinced in the advice given to the highest types of ganikas by the eroticists on how to spend their earnings. They were to build temples, swimming pools and gardens; give a thousand cows to different Brahmans; carry on the worship of the gods, and to celebrate festivals in their honor; and to perform all the religious vows that were within their means.

Across the centuries the ganikas became more numerous and with their increasing numbers developed a complex body of regulations and duties. So important had they already become in Vatsya Yana's time that he could say: "A public woman, endowed with a good disposition, beauty, and other winning qualities, and also well versed and proficient in all the sixty-four arts of love obtains the name of a ganika, or public woman of high quality, and receives a seat of honor in an assemblage of men. She is moreover always respected by the king, praised by learned men, and her favor sought by all—an object of universal regard."

The Ganika or Glorified Prostitution

The sixty-four arts of love to which Vatsya Yana refers are not to be confused with the sixty-four social arts or with the preliminaries to possession. There are an additional sixty-four arts that are to be learned by the prostitute before she can be called a ganika. Kshemendra in his *Kalavilasa* describes these arts as "enchanting, fickle, rich in tempestuous floods, and which surge in the depths of the heart of the ganika like waves in the ocean."

The following are the sixty-four arts of love to be learned by the ganika:

1. *The Art of Prostitution*
2. *The Art of Dance*
3. *The Art of Song*
4. *The Art of the Slanting Gaze*
5. *The Art of Recognizing Love*
6. *The Art of Holding Fast*
7. *The Art of Securing Friends*
8. *The Art of Betraying Friends*
9. *The Art of Drinking*
10. *The Art of Pleasure*
11. *The Art of Special Embraces*
12. *The Art of Kissing*
13. *The Art of All the other Caresses*
14. *The Art of Shameless Impetuosity*
15. *The Art of Disarrangement*
16. *The Art of Simulating Jealousy*

17. *The Art of Simulating Discord*
18. *The Art of Crying*
19. *The Art of Pride*
20. *The Art of Self-denial*
21. *The Art of Perspiring*
22. *The Art of Cheating*
23. *The Art of Trembling*
24. *The Art of Sighing*
25. *The Art of Beautifying Oneself*
26. *The Art of Simulating Impotency*
27. *The Art of Folding the Eye-lids*
28. *The Art of Simulating Death*
29. *The Art of Showing Passion*
30. *The Art of Peremptoriness*
31. *The Art of Striking*
32. *The Art of Wrath*
33. *The Art of Quarreling with One's Mother*
34. *The Art of Visiting the Home of the Love*
35. *The Art of Participating in Festivals*
36. *The Art of Accepting*
37. *The Art of Personality*
38. *The Art of Playing*
39. *The Art of the Prince among Thieves*
40. *The Art of Courage*
41. *The Art of Humility*
42. *The Art of Simulating Poverty*
43. *The Art of Simulating Pain*
44. *The Art of Rubbing*
45. *The Art of Simulating Sleep*

The Ganika or Glorified Prostitution

46. *The Art of Simulating the Monthlies*
47. *The Art of Ignoring the Lover*
48. *The Art of Bolting*
49. *The Art of Dismissing Visitors*
50. *The Art of Boasting of Former Lovers*
51. *The Art of Searching for Former Lovers*
52. *The Art of Conduct with Former Lovers*
53. *The Art of Retaining Former Lovers*
54. *The Art of Residing in Holy Shrines*
55. *The Art of Enjoyment in Holy Shrines*
56. *The Art of Using Love-charms*
57. *The Art of Understanding Arbors*
58. *The Art of Dyeing the Hair*
59. *The Art of Adaptation to Foreign Customs*
60. *The Art of Impersonating Another Woman*
61. *The Art of Contracting the Vaginal Muscle*
62. *The Art of Intellectual Recreations*
63. *The Art of Simulating Virginity*
64. *The Art of the Procuress*

Naturally the eroticists required that the ganika possess exceptional traits of character, temperament and intelligence in addition to being well versed in the above arts. Among these qualities, the most important were: She should be possessed of beauty and amiability with auspicious body-marks. She should have a liking for good qualities in other people, as also a liking for wealth. She should take delight in sexual unions resulting from love, and should be of a firm mind, and of the same class as the man with whom she indulges in congress. She should always be anxious to acquire experience and knowledge, be free from avarice, and always be fond of social gatherings and the arts.

These qualities are in addition to the usual traits of a ganika, to wit:

To be possessed of intelligence, good disposition, and good manners; to be straightforward in behavior, and to be grateful; to consider the future before doing anything; to be active, of consistent behavior, and to know the proper times and places for all occasions; to speak always without meanness, loud laughter, malignity, anger, avarice, dullness; to possess a thorough knowledge of the *Kama Sutra,* and to be skilled in all the arts which it teaches.

By intercourse with men ganikas obtain pleasure as well as their own maintenance. When a ganika unites with a man for love, the action is natural; but when she resorts to him for the purpose of obtaining money, her action is considered artificial or forced. Even in this latter case, however, she should conduct herself as if her love were natural because men repose confidence in those women who seem to love them. In making known her love to the man, she should manifest entire freedom from avarice and abstain from acquiring money from him by unlawful means.

A ganika, well dressed and wearing her ornaments, should sit or stand at the door of her house, and without exposing herself too much, should look on the public road so as to be seen by the passersby; for she is like an object on view for sale. She should form friendships with the following persons:

The guards of the town, or the police
The officers of the courts of justice
Astrologers
Men who have power in the community
Teachers of the sixty-four arts
Pithamardas or confidants
Vitas or parasites
Vidushkas or jesters
Perfumers
Venders of spirits
Barbers

The above list may be supplemented by other persons if they are essential in aiding her to acquire some particular object. The ganika may also become intimate with certain men from whom she may wish to obtain money:

Men of independent income
Men who are free from any ties

The Hindu Art of Love

Men who hold places of authority under the king
Men who consider themselves handsome
Men who are always praising themselves
A eunuch who wishes to be thought a man
One who is naturally liberal
One who has influence with the king or his ministers
One who is always fortunate
One who is guarded by the members of his caste
An only son whose father is wealthy
An ascetic who is internally troubled with desire

To the above list may be added such men as will bestow upon the ganikas fame and honor. With these she may have intercourse for love or money, since they are the highest of nayakas.

The following are the men with whom the ganikas should never have congress: One who is consumptive; one who is sickly; one whose mouth contains worms; one whose breath smells like human excrement; one whose wife is dear to him; one who speaks harshly; one who is always suspicious; one who is avaricious; one who is pitiless; one who is a thief; one who is self-conceited; one who hankers after sorcery; one who will betray even his friends for money; and lastly, one who is extremely bashful.

Ancient authors are of the opinion that numerous motives operate in the choices of men by ganikas.

The Ganika or Glorified Prostitution

These motives range from love, pleasure, and compassion, to curiosity, fear, and money. Vatsya Yana condensed the list to desire of wealth, freedom from misfortune, and love as being the only causes which lead ganikas to surrender their charms and persons to men.

A ganika should not sacrifice money to her love, because money is the prime factor in her life. Yet there are many individual exceptions to this rule. Moreover, even though she be invited by any man for congress, she should not at once consent because men are apt to despise things which are too easily acquired.

On such occasions she should first send the shampooers, singers, and jesters who may be in her service, or in their absence the pithamardas and confidants to find out the state of his feelings. In this wise she will ascertain whether the man is pure or impure, affected or reverse, capable of attachment or indifferent, liberal or niggardly. Should she find him to her liking, she must then employ the vita and others to attach him to her.

Accordingly, the pithamarda should bring the man to her house under the pretence of witnessing fights of quails, cocks, and rams, of hearing the starling talk, or of attending some other spectacle.

Once the man visits her, the ganika should arouse his curiosity and love by an affectionate gift, telling him that it was especially designed for his use. She should also entertain him for a long time with amusing stories and other pastimes. When he goes away she should frequently send to him a female attendant, skilled in witty conversation. She should also visit him from time to time under the pretence of business, accompanied by the pithamarda.

The axiom of the Hindus is that *men want pleasure while women want money*. Hence the eroticists counsel the ganika how to obtain money from lovers in every possible way.

When a ganika is able to realize much money every day, by reason of many customers, she should not confine herself to a single lover; under such circumstances, she should fix her rate for one night, after considering the place, the season, and the condition of the man, also having regard to her own high qualities and good looks, and after comparing her rates with those of other ganikas. She can inform her lovers, friends, and acquaintances about these changes. If however she can obtain a large amount from a single lover, she may resort to him alone, and live with him as wife.

The sages are of the opinion that when a ganika

has the opportunity of equal sums from two lovers at the same time, the preference should be given to the more vigorous one. But Vatsya Yana characteristically suggests that the preference should be given to the one who gives her money because it cannot be taken back like some other things; it can be easily received and is also the means of fulfilling her tastes. Of such payments as money, silver, copper, bell metal, iron, pots, furniture, beds, outer garments, under vestments, fragrant substances, vessels made of gourds, ghee, oil, corn, and cattle, the first, that is, money, is superior to all the others.

When the same efforts are required to tempt two lovers, or when equal payments are to be got from them, the choice should be made by the advice of a friend, or it may be determined by their personal qualities, or from the signs of good or bad fortune which may be connected with them.

When there are two lovers, one of whom is attached to the ganika, and the other is simply generous, the sages assert that preference should be given to the generous lover, but artful Vatsya Yana says that the one who is really attached to the ganika should be preferred.

A comprehensive classification of the relative advantages and disadvantages derived from any affair

has been specified for the conduct of ganikas by most
of the classic eroticists. Two systems are more widely
followed than the rest, these being the regulations
laid down by Uddalika and Babhravya. They are too
detailed and divided to deserve extensive consideration here though an explanatory word or two is really
necessary.

Whenever a ganika gives herself to a man, whatever the motive or circumstances, she derives some
advantage or disadvantage or combination of both.
The advantages are grouped under three heads: advantages of wealth, of religious merit, or of pleasure.
The disadvantages are also three, similar to the
above. The combinations of advantage and disadvantage are six, being variations of the above two
groups.

When a ganika abandons her present lover after
all his wealth is exhausted, she may then consider
her reunion with a former lover. But she should
return to him only if he has acquired additional
wealth, or is still wealthy, and if he is still attached
to her. But if this man is living with some other
woman she should deliberate carefully before she
acts.

Now such a man must be in one of the six following conditions:

The Ganika or Glorified Prostitution

1. *He may have left the ganika of his own accord, as well as one or more women since.*
2. *He may have been driven away by several women.*
3. *He may have left the ganika of his own accord, and been driven away by the last woman.*
4. *He may have left the ganika of his own accord, and be living with another woman.*
5. *He may have been driven away by the ganika and left the last woman of his own accord.*
6. *He may have been driven away by the ganika and be living with another woman.*

In the first case, he should not be considered on account of his fickleness.

In the second case, if he has been driven away by the last woman for mercenary reasons, he should be considered for he is likely to become more generous than ever to spite her. But if he has been driven away by the woman on account of his poverty or stinginess, he should not be considered.

In the third case, if he agrees to return to the ganika and give her plenty of money beforehand, he should be considered.

In the fourth case, the ganika should ascertain if he left her out of love for some other woman, and was disappointed. If so, the ganika should go back to him only if he will pay her handsomely for his maltreatment.

In the fifth case, the ganika should carefully deliberate if he still cares for her or whether he is revengeful for her treatment of him. If the former, she should re-unite herself with him.

In the sixth case, only if the man makes overtures to the ganika, should she consider him, and then only if certain definite advantages of wealth, religious merit, or pleasure will result from a second union with him.

Once a ganika resolves to live again with a former lover, she should send her servants to him to explain that his former expulsion from her house was caused by the wickedness of her mother; that she loved him as much as ever at that time but had to defer to her mother's will; that she dislikes her present lover. In addition to this, the ganika's servants should recall to him the many scenes and memories of their mutual love and say that the ganika always alludes to those occasions. They should also refer to some special quality which he possesses as a lover, such as his way of kissing her or his favorite manner of congress with her.

A ganika should always know the disposition of her lover towards her, from his changes of temper, manner, and facial expression. She should know that the behavior of a waning lover is as follows:

The Ganika or Glorified Prostitution

He gives her less than she asks for or something else.
He keeps her in hopes by promises.
He pretends to do one thing and does another.
He does not fulfill her amorous desires.
He forgets his promises or does something else.
He speaks with his own servants in a mysterious way.
He spends the night in some other house secretly.
He speaks with the attendants of a former mistress.

When a ganika finds that her lover's disposition toward her is changing, she should attempt to obtain all his most valuable possessions before he becomes aware of her intentions, and allow a pretended creditor to take them away forcibly in payment of some debt. After this deception, if the lover is rich, and has always behaved generously towards her, she should treat him with respect; but if he is poor she should get rid of him as soon as possible.

The following are the best means of getting rid of a lover:

Seeking the company of more intelligent men
Expressing dissatisfaction with his manner of congress
Refusing him her mouth to kiss
Refusing access to her jaghana
Manifesting dislike for marks made by his nails
Not responding to his caresses
Lying inert while congress is in session

The Hindu Art of Love

Expressing desire for congress when he is fatigued
Ridiculing his attachment to her
Pretending drowsiness when he begins to embrace her
Going out visiting when he desires to enjoy her
Deliberately misconstruing his words
Laughing inopportunely at his jokes
Exchanging meaningful glances with her attendants
Interrupting him in the middle of his stories
Making side remarks about him to her attendants
Requesting impossible caresses
And, finally, dismissing him

When a ganika is living as a wife with her lover, she should behave like a chaste woman and do everything to please him. Her principal duty is to give him pleasure, and simulate love, but she must never become attached to him genuinely. She should also strive to retain his love by:

Expressing wonder at his knowledge of sexual inter-course
Learning from him the sixty-four kinds of pleasures mentioned by Babhravya
Continually practising the art of love as taught by him, and according to his taste
Caressing him whenever he requests her
Kissing and embracing him when he is asleep
Expressing a curiosity to see his wives

The Ganika or Glorified Prostitution

Feigning jealousy of the nail and teeth marks made on
his body by other women
Remaining silent when he is intoxicated
Not acting too familiarly with him
Placing his hands on her loins, bosom, and forehead,
and falling asleep after thrilling to his touch
Sitting on his lap and falling asleep in this position

Such is the manner of a ganika who lives with a
man as his wife, as set forth by Dattaka. All other
eroticists have compiled similar studies of the behavior of ganikas under all conditions of love and
life.

Rules for the daughters of ganikas have also been
recorded by all the eroticists, though these are comparatively simple and few. When the daughter of a
ganika arrives at the age of puberty, the mother
should assemble several young men of the same disposition and training as her daughter, and offer her
in marriage to any of them for a certain small sum.

When the daughter of a ganika is thus given to a
man the ties of marriage are observed for one year,
and after that she may do as she chooses. But even
after the end of the year, if she should be invited on
occasion by her first husband to spend the night with
him, she should do so unless exceptional circumstances interfere. This mode of temporary marriage

among the daughters of ganikas is really an apprenticeship for the purpose of becoming adept in the Art of Love. It is tolerated as a matter of common conduct in India and is but a natural offshoot of the child-marriage system there.

The entire subject of the ganika, her place, power and acceptance in Hindu life, is one of the most devious departments of Indic esoterica. It is conditioned by so many peculiarities of faith and tradition, and imbued with so many hypocritical shams that no matter how exhaustively one treats the subject, and however accurately, can one depict the ganika faithfully without endless qualification and quibble. Recognizing this fact and aware of our own disapprobation of the ganika and the vicious system which she represents, we have emphasized in this chapter the opinions of only the most important Hindu sages who have dealt at length with the subject: Babhravya, Dattaka, Bharata, Vatsya Yana, Uddalika, Kshemendra, Katya Yana, and others.

X

Eunuchs and Kings as Lovers

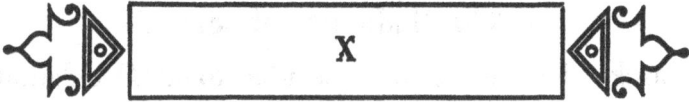

EUNUCHS
AND
KINGS
AS
LOVERS

Although homosexuality and lesbianism play very small parts in the sexual life of Hindus, the role of the eunuch is a very important one. The Hindus call the eunuch a prostitute and permit him many of the rights and privileges accorded to the ganika. This may appear peculiar to our Occidental concepts but a knowledge of Hindu social and sexual life more than justifies such a seeming misnomer. His duties are not so varied nor his activities so multiple as those of the ganika but they are sufficient to identify the eunuch as a high-class specialized prostitute.

In India there are two kinds of eunuchs, those disguised as males, and those disguised as females. Eunuchs disguised as females imitate feminine dress, speech, gestures, timidity, softness and bashfulness. The intimacies usually reserved for the female jaghana, or central portions of the body of women, are transferred to the mouths of these eunuchs and this is called *auparishtaka.*

This practise appears to have been prevalent in India from a very ancient time. The Sushruta, a work on medicine some two thousand years old, describes the wounding of the lingam with the teeth as one of the causes of a disease dealt with in that work. Traces of this practise are found as far back as the eighth century, for various kinds of the auparishtaka are represented in the sculptures of many shaiva temples at Bhuvaneshwara, near Cuttack in Orissa, and which were built during that period. From the prevalence of such sculptures it seems that this practise was popular in that part of the country at that time. It is assuredly not so prevalent now in India although the practise of sodomy, which was introduced in the Mohammedan period, still endures though not so widespread as elsewhere.

The eunuchs disguised as females derive both their imaginative pleasure and their livelihood from this perversion of congress. These and other practises lead to their similarity of life with the general run of ganikas.

Eunuchs disguised as males keep their desires secret and do not parade openly. They sit by the windows watching the passersby—the usual custom among the Hindu prostitutes—as do their quasi-sisters under the skin. When they choose legitimate vocations, they become barbers or shampooers. Under the pretence of shampooing, this type of eunuch embraces and draws towards himself the thighs of the man whom he is shampooing, afterwards casually touching the thighs and his jaghana. If after these obvious overtures, the man does not request the eunuch to proceed, the latter does so of his own accord and begins the congress. If, however, he is ordered by the man to do so, he pretends to dispute with him, and consents at last only with difficulty.

Among the legitimate sisters of the eunuch, the auparishtaka is practised only by unchaste and wanton women, female attendants and serving maids, in short, those who are unmarried and who live by shampooing.

The Acharyas, the ancient and venerable sages, hold that the auparishtaka is the work of a dog and not of a man, because it is a low practise and not sanctioned by the Holy Writ, and because the man himself suffers through such contact with the mouths of eunuchs and women. But Vatsya Yana says that the sanctions of the Holy Writ do not affect those who resort to prostitutes, and that the law prohibits the practise of the auparishtaka with married women only. To counter the last objection, possible injury to the man, he advances remedies and cures for the quick alleviation of any such injury.

The male servants of some men indulge in the auparishtaka with their masters. It is also mutually practised by some citizens who know each other well. Many ganikas become so passionately attached to this method that they abandon men of good qualities, liberal and wise, and become attached to low persons, such as slaves and elephant drivers. Fortunately, such lasciviousness is not common.

The practise of the auparishtaka is really not allowed by the eroticists and is strongly condemned in the case of a learned Brahman, a minister that carries on the business of a state, or a man of good reputation. This mode of congress seems to be principally a matter of geography. The Hindus of Eastern India despise the perversion and do not resort to women who practise it. The Ahichhatra resort to such women but do not indulge in extreme limits. The Saketa practise all variations of the auparishtaka with these women and are ever on the lookout for new perversions.

In many parts of India the eunuch is regarded as a preliminary prostitute, that is, he is used by the man as a kind of aphrodisiac. Before the woman appears, the man—especially if he is old, feeble, semi-impotent or impotent—calls a eunuch to his house. The eunuch proceeds to shampoo him thoroughly; then he rubs his body forcefully and violently for a long time, until the man feels the flush of heat come over him. The auparishtaka is not usually practised except in severe cases.

Very curious indeed are these two tasks of the eunuch, due in a large measure to the desire of the Hindus to enjoy a particular protagonist for a particular duty. It is this desire which has led to the glorification of prostitution, and the Hindu specialization in all the arts and intimacies of the embrace. Even the lot of the common, low-caste prostitute is less disdainful in India than in Europe or America.

The caste system being so powerful in India it is but natural for the eroticists to devote much study to the proper conduct of high officials. We shall allow the eroticists to speak for themselves on this phase of the subject.

Kings and their ministers have no access to the abodes of others, and moreover their mode of living is constantly imitated by the people. Thus, persons in authority should not perform any improper act in public, as such actions are most unworthy of their position and most deserving of censure. But if they find that some such action is necessary, they should make use of the following proper means and opportunities.

The chief of the village, the King's officer employed there, and the man whose business it is to superintend the gleaning of corn, can seduce female villagers simply by asking them. It is on this account that these women are considered unchaste by voluptuaries.

The union of the above mentioned men with such women takes place on the occasions of unpaid labor, of filling the granaries in their houses, of cleaning the houses, of working in the fields, and of purchasing cotton, wool, flax, hemp, and thread, and at the season of the purchase, sale, and exchange of various other articles.

In the same way the superintendents of the cow pens enjoy the women in the cow pens; and officers who have the superintendence of widows, of women who are without support, and of women who have left their husbands, have sexual intercourse with these women.

Amorous men accomplish their object by wandering at night in the village, while villagers also unite with the wives of their sons, being much alone with them. Lastly, the superintendents of markets find much to do with female villagers when the latter make purchases in the market.

We have explicit information as to how the King shall best proceed in enjoying a woman with whom he has fallen in love. During the festival of the eighth moon, that is during the bright half of the month of Nargashirsha, as also during the moonlight festival of the month of Kartika, and the spring festival of Chaitra, the women of cities and towns generally visit the women of the King's harem in the royal palace. These visitors go to the several apartments of the women of the harem, as they are acquainted with them, and pass the night in conversation and in proper sports and amusements, and leave in the morning.

On such occasions, a female attendant of the King, previously acquainted with the woman whom the King desires, should loiter about and accost this woman when she sets out to go home, and induce her to come and see the interesting trophies in the palace. Accordingly, she should show her the bower of the coral creeper, the garden house with its floor inlaid with precious stones, the bower of grapes, the building on the water, the secret passages in the wall of the palace, the pictures, the sporting animals, the machines, the birds, and the cages with lions and tigers. After this, the royal intermediary should tell her about the King's love for her, and should rhapsodize on the good fortune attendant upon her union with him, threatening her at the time to secrecy. If the woman does not accept the offer, she should be conciliated with handsome presents, befitting the position of the King, and should be dismissed with great affection.

A second method: Having made the acquaintance of the husband of the woman whom the King desires, the wives of the King should get the wife to pay them a visit in the harem, and on this occasion a female attendant of the palace, having been sent there, should act as above described.

A third method: One of the King's wives should become acquainted with the woman whom the King desires by sending one of the female attendants to her, who should, on their becoming more intimate, induce the woman to come and see the royal abode. Afterwards when she has visited the harem and acquired confidence, a female confidant of the King should be sent there and act as above described.

A fourth method: One of the King's wives should invite the woman whom the monarch desires to the palace, to witness the practise of the art in which the King's wife may be skilled. After she has come to the harem, a female attendant of the King should be sent there and act as before described.

A fifth method: A female beggar, in league with one of the King's wives, should say to the woman whom he desires, and whose husband may have lost his wealth or may have some cause to fear the King: "This wife of the King has influence over him, and she is moreover naturally kind-hearted. We must therefore go to her in this matter. I shall arrange for your entrance into the harem, and she will do away with all danger and fear from the King." If the woman accepts this offer, the female beggar should take her several times to the harem, and the King's wife there should promise her protection. After this, when the woman, delighted with her reception and promise of protection, again goes to the harem, a female servant of the palace should be in readiness to act as above directed.

What has been said about the wife of one who has some cause to fear the King, applies also to the wives of those who seek service under the King, or who are oppressed by the royal ministers, or who are poor, or who are not satisfied with their position, or who are desirous of gaining the King's favor, or who wish to become famous among the people, or who are oppressed by the members of their own caste, or who want to injure their caste fellows, or who are spies of the King, or who have any other similar object to attain.

Lastly: If the woman desired by the King be living with some person who is not her husband, then the King should cause her to be arrested and, having made her a slave on account of her crime, should place her in his harem.

The above mentioned ways of seducing the wives of other men are chiefly practised in the palaces of Kings. For there is an unwritten law that a King must never enter the abode of another person, probably because Abhira, the King of the Kottas, was killed by a washerman while in the house of another, and in the same way Jayasana, the King of the Cashis, was slain by the commander of his cavalry.

Nevertheless, according to the customs of some countries there are facilities for Kings in making love to the wives of other men. Thus in the country of the Andras, the newly married daughters of the people enter the King's harem with some presents on the tenth day of their marriage, and having been enjoyed by the King are then dismissed. In the country of the Vatsagulamas, the wives of the chief ministers approach the King at night to serve his royal wishes. In the country of the Vaidarbhas, the beautiful wives of the inhabitants pass a month in the King's harem under the pretence of affection for the King. In the country of the Aparatakas, the people give their beautiful wives as presents to the ministers and the Kings. And lastly, in the country of the Saurashtras, the women of the city and country enter the royal harem for the King's pleasure either together or separately.

Thus it will be palpable that the King claims everybody for his private pleasures even though his harem is always well stocked and sufficient unto his days. The women of the harem are strictly

guarded and must go many a day unappeased because their royal husband must be divided among
so many wives. For this reason they pleasure one
another in various ways. They dress the daughters
of their nurses, or their female friends, or their female attendants, like men and resort to lewd acts
by means of bulbs, roots, and fruits having the
form of a lingam, or they sometimes employ the
statue of a male figure whose lingam is prominent.

Some Kings who are compassionate take certain
medicines to enable them to enjoy many wives in
one night, simply for the purpose of satisfying the
desire of their women, even when their own passions
are temporarily quiescent. Others enjoy with great
affection only such wives as they are particularly
fond of, while still others embrace them in rotation,
according as the due turn of each wife arrives.

Oddly enough, the eroticists exhibit no preference in bestowing their sage advice. They record
how the King must go about getting the wives of
others. Similarly, they record how men must go
about getting the wives of the King. Truly a Hindu
roundelay! This periphrastic prostitution is arrived
at in the following manners:

The ladies of the royal harem, by means of their
female attendants, generally get men into their

apartments in the disguise or dress of women. Their female attendants, and the daughters of their nurses who are acquainted with their secrets, should exert themselves in getting men to come to the harem by describing the facilities of entering and leaving the palace, the large size of the premises, the careless-ness of the sentinels, and the irregularities of the attendants of the royal wives. But these women should never induce a man to enter the harem by telling him falsehoods, for that would probably lead to his destruction.

As for the man himself, he had better not enter a royal harem, however accessible, on account of the numerous disasters to which he may be exposed there. But if determined to enter it, he should first ascertain whether there is an easy exit, whether it is closely surrounded by the pleasure garden, whether it has separate enclosures belonging to it, whether the sentinels are careless, whether the King has gone abroad, and then, when he is solicited by the women of the harem, he should carefully observe the layout, and enter only by the way pointed out to him.

If he is able to manage it, he should visit the harem every day, and under some pretext make friends with the sentinels and manifest a fondness for the female attendants. He may acquaint the latter with his design and express his regret to them at not being able to obtain the object of his desire. He should also arrange for a female procuress who has access to the harem, and he must learn to recognize the emissaries of the King.

When a procuress has no access to the harem, the man should stand somewhere in view of the lady whom he loves and whom he is anxious to enjoy. If such a spot is occupied by the King's sentinels he should then disguise himself as a female attendant of the lady who has occasion to pass that spot. When she looks at him he should let her know his feelings by outward signs and gestures and should show her pictures with double meanings, chaplets of flowers, and rings. He should carefully mark the answer she gives, whether by word or by sign or by gesture, and should then make efforts to gain an entrance into the harem. If he is certain that she will visit some particular place, he should conceal himself there, and at the appointed time should enter along with her as one of her guards. Or he may enter the harem during the moonlight festivals when the female attendants of the harem are all busily occupied.

In general the entrance of young men into harems, and their exit from them, takes place when deliveries are made, or when drinking festivals are going on, or when the female attendants are in a hurry, or when the residences of some of the royal ladies are being changed, or when the King's wives go to fairs, or when they enter the palace on their return from them, or finally, when the King is absent on a long pilgrimage.

The women of the royal harem know one another's secrets, and all having similar clandestine passions, they give assistance to one another. A young man who enjoys all of them, as is sometimes the case, can continue his illicit pleasures with them so long as it is kept quiet, and is not known abroad.

Upon this subject of harem intrigues, the Hindu eroticists have a great deal to say. They appear to lay particular stress upon the differences of harem life in various parts of India, some of which are worthy of mention at this point.

In the country of the Aparatakas the royal ladies are not well protected and consequently many young men are passed into the harem by women who have access to the royal palace. The wives of the King of the Ahira country accomplish their privacies with the sentinels in the harem who bear the name of Kshtriyas. The royal ladies in the country of the Vatsyagulmas permit handsome lovers to enter the harem disguised as female messengers. In the country of the Vaidarbhas the sons of the royal ladies enter the royal harem when they please, and enjoy the women, with the exception of their own mothers. In the Stri-rajya the wives of the King are enjoyed by his caste fellows and relations.

In the Ganda country the royal wives are enjoyed by Brahmans, friends, servants and slaves. In the Samdhava country, servants, foster children, and other men of low degree enjoy the women of the harem. In the country of the Haimavatas adventurous citizens bribe the sentinels and enter the harem. In the country of the Vabyas and the Kalmyas, Brahmans, with the knowledge of the King, enter the harem under the pretence of giving flowers to the ladies and speak with them from behind curtains, and afterwards partake in other liberties. Finally, the women in the harem of the King of the Prachyas conceal one young man in the harem for every batch of nine or ten women.

There is a great deal more to be said on the place of harem sexuality in India but we do not pursue the subject any further as it would be outside the borders of the Hindu Art of Love. Even the most venerable Hindu sages condone all kinds of immoral harem intrigues upon the implicit assumption that since harem life itself is based upon sexual excesses, further liberties should be permitted within its confines than elsewhere. Accordingly, a great many Sanscrit works prevail which attempt to help the nayaka to cuckold Kings and important officials who rule over large harems. From the point of view of Christian morals, all such works are wholly reprehensible and can be explained only on the basis of a complicated philosophy of love in which black is white and wrong is right.

XI

The Private Conduct of the Wife

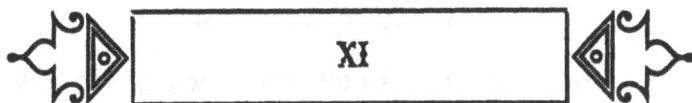

THE
PRIVATE
CONDUCT
OF
THE
WIFE

We have already considered the eroticists' detailed information to the woman on the safest means of outwitting her husband. In this chapter we shall concern ourselves with a picture of the life of a virtuous woman and of her private conduct.

The Hindu Art of Love

According to the Hindu lawgivers, a virtuous woman who has affection for her husband should act in conformity with his wishes as if he were a divine being, and with his consent should take upon herself the whole care of his family. She should keep the house well cleaned, arrange flowers of various kinds in different parts of it, and polish the floor. She should surround the house with a garden, and keep in readiness in it everything required for daily sacrifices. Moreover, she should herself revere the sanctuary of the Household Gods, for says Gonardiya, "Nothing so much attracts the heart of an householder to his wife as her careful observance of the things mentioned above."

Towards the parents, relations, friends, sisters and servants of her husband, she should behave as they deserve. In the garden she should plant beds of green vegetables, bunches of sugar cane, and clumps of the fig tree, the mustard plant, and the parsley plant. Clusters of various flowers such as the jasmine, the yellow amaranth, the china rose and others, should likewise be planted. She should also have seats and arbors built in the garden, in the middle of which a well and swimming pool should be dug.

The wife should always avoid the company of female beggars, female buddhist mendicants, unchaste and roguish women, female fortune tellers and witches. As regards meals, she should always consider what her husband likes and dislikes, what things are good for him, and what are injurious to him. When she hears the sounds of his homecoming footsteps she should get up at once, and be ready to do whatever he may command her, ordering her female servant to wash his feet or to wash them herself.

When going anywhere with her husband she should put on her ornaments, and without his consent she should neither give nor accept invitations, or attend marriages and sacrifices, or sit in the company of female friends, or visit the temples of the Gods. If she wishes to engage in any kind of game or sport, she must not do it against his will. In the same way she must always sit down after him, and get up before him, and should never awaken him when he is asleep. The kitchen should be situated in a quiet and retired spot, so as not to be accessible to strangers, and should always look clean.

In the event of any misconduct on the part of her husband, she should not blame him excessively, though she be a little displeased. She should not use abusive language towards him, but should rebuke him with conciliatory words, whether he be in the company of friends or alone. Moreover she should not be a scold, for says Gonardiya, "There is nothing more offensive to a husband than this trait in a wife." She should avoid vulgar language, sulky looks, speaking aside, standing in the doorway, looking at passersby, conversing in pleasure groves, and remaining in a lonely place for a long time. She must always keep her body, her teeth, her hair, and other parts of her body, sweet and clean.

When the wife wants to approach her husband in private, her dress should consist of many ornaments, various kinds of flowers, a cloth decorated with different colors, and some sweet-smelling ointments or unguents. But her every-day dress should be composed of a thin, close-textured cloth, a few ornaments and flowers, and a little scent, not too much. She should also observe the fasts and vows of her husband, and when he attempts to dissuade her from following his example, she should insist on his permission to the contrary.

At appropriate times of the year, and when they happen to be cheap, she should buy earth, bamboos, firewood, skins and iron pots, salt and oil. Fragrant substances, vessels made of certain medicines and other constant requisites should be obtained when required and kept in a secret place of the house. The seeds of the radish, the potato, the beet, the egg-plant, the pumpkin, the sandalwood, the garlic plant, the onion, and other vegetables, should be bought and sown during their proper seasons.

The wife should not inform strangers of the amount of her wealth, nor the secrets which her husband has confided in her. She should attempt to surpass the women of her own rank in cleverness, knowledge of cookery, and manner of serving her husband. The expenditures of the year should be determined by the earnings. The milk left over after meals should be turned into ghee or clear butter. Oil and sugar should be prepared at home; spinning and weaving should also be done there; and a supply of rope and cord and barks of trees for twisting into ropes, should always be on hand. Among the duties of the wife are the pounding and cleaning of rice, and utilizing the chaff in some way. She should pay the salaries of the servants, look after the tilling of the fields, the keeping of the flocks and herds, superintend the construction of vehicles, and take care of the rams, cocks, quails, parrots, starlings, cuckoos, peacocks, monkeys and deer.

The friends of her husband she should welcome by presenting them with flowers, ointment, incense, betel leaves and betel nut. Her father-in-law and mother-in-law she should treat as they deserve, always remaining dependent on their will, never contradicting them, speaking to them in few and kindly words, not laughing loudly in their presence, and acting with their friends and enemies as with her own. In addition to the above she should not be vain, or too much taken up with her own enjoyments. She should be liberal towards her servants, and reward them on holidays and festivals; but she should not give away anything without first making it known to her husband.

During the absence of her husband on a journey, the virtuous woman should wear only her auspicious ornaments, and observe the fasts in honor of the gods. While anxious to hear news of her husband, she should continue to look after her household affairs as usual. She should sleep near the older women of the house and make herself agreeable to them. She should attend to all the little things which her husband is fond of. She must not visit the homes of her relatives except on occasions of joy or sorrow, and then she should go in her usual travelling dress, accompanied by her husband's servants, and not remain there too long.

When her husband returns from his journey, she should receive him at first in her ordinary clothes,

so that he may know in what way she has lived
during his absence, and should bring him gifts as
well as articles for the worship of the Deity.

The role of the Hindu wife becomes proportion-
ately more complicated when there are several wives,
which is very frequently the case. As usual, the
classic eroticists have much to say upon this matter.
According to them, there are five major conditions
underlying a Hindu's remarriage during the lifetime
of his wife:

The folly or ill-temper of the wife
The husband's dislike of her
The want of offspring
The continual birth of daughters only
The incontinence of the wife

The first wife has precedence over all other
wives, and her first-born son over his half-brothers.
As for the secondary wives, it is difficult to dis-
tinguish between these and concubines, especially
when the former have borne no male offspring, or
when the husband is in love with one of his concubines.

From the very beginning a wife should endeavor
to attract the heart of her husband by manifesting
her devotion continually. If however she bears him

no children she must herself tell him to marry another woman. And when the second wife is married,
and brought into the house, the first wife must give
her a position almost equal to her own, and treat
her as a sister.

In the morning the elder wife should forcibly
make the younger one decorate herself in the presence of their husband, and should not mind at all
the husband's favoritism to the latter. If the younger
wife does anything to displease her husband the
elder one should not neglect her, but should always
be ready to give her the most careful advice, and
should teach her how to perform certain confidential
duties in the presence of her husband. She should
treat the children of the younger wife as her own,
she should look upon her attendants with more regard than upon her own servants, she should cherish
her friends with love and kindness, and her relatives
with great honor.

When there are many other wives besides herself,
the eldest wife should associate with the one who is
immediately next to her in rank and age, and should
induce the latter to quarrel with the present favorite. After this, having brought all the wives together,
she should get them to denounce the favorite as a
scheming and wicked woman, without however com-

mitting herself in any way. If the favorite wife happens to quarrel with the husband then the eldest wife should take her part and give her false encouragement, thus causing the quarrel to be intensified. If there be only a slight quarrel between the two, the eldest wife should do all she can to work it up into a larger quarrel. But if, after all this, she finds that her husband still continues to love his favorite wife, she should then change her tactics, and endeavor to bring about a conciliation between them, so as to avoid her husband's displeasure.

The youngest wife should regard the eldest wife of her husband as her mother and should not give anything away, even to her own parents, without the latter's knowledge. She should tell her everything about herself, and not approach her husband without her permission. Whatever is told her by the eldest wife must be kept in strictest confidence, and she should take better care of the children of the senior wife than of her own. When alone with her husband she should serve him well, but should not tell him of the jealousy she suffers from the existence of a rival wife. She may also obtain secretly from her husband some tokens of his affection for her, and may tell him that she lives only for him, and for his love. She should never reveal her love for her husband, nor her husband's love for her to any person, either in pride or in anger, for a wife that reveals the secrets of her husband is despised by him. As for seeking to obtain the love of her husband, Gonardiya says that it should always be done in private, for fear of the eldest wife. If the latter is disliked by her husband, or is childless, the youngest wife should sympathize with her, and should ask her husband to do the same, but should surpass her rival in leading the life of a chaste woman.

The eroticists hold that a widow in poor circumstances or of a weak nature may ally herself again with a man. The followers of Babhravya say that a virgin should not marry a person whom she may be obliged to leave on account of his bad character. Gonardiya is of the opinion that as the cause of a widow's remarriage is her desire for happiness, and as happiness is secured by the possession of excellent qualities in her husband, joined to a love of enjoyment, it is better therefore to secure a person endowed with such qualities in the first instance. Vatsya Yana however holds that a widow may marry any person she likes and who she thinks will suit her.

At the time of her marriage the widow should obtain from her husband sufficient money to cover the

cost of drinking parties and picnics with her relatives, and of giving them and her friends kindly
gifts. In the same way, she may wear either her husband's ornaments or her own. As to the gift of affection mutually exchanged between the husband and
herself, there is no fixed rule about this. If she leaves
her husband after marriage of her own accord, she
should restore to him whatever he may have given
her, with the exception of these mutual gifts. If
however she is driven out of the house by her husband she is not obliged to return any of his gifts to
him.

After her marriage she should live in the house of
her husband like one of the chief members of the
family, but should treat the other ladies of the family
with kindness, the servants with generosity, and all
the friends of the house with familiarity and good
temper. She should attempt to show that she is better
acquainted with the sixty-four arts than the other
ladies of the house, and in any quarrels with her
husband she should not rebuke him severely, but in
private do everything that he wishes, and make use
of the sixty-four ways of amorous caresses. She
should give presents to the children of her husband's
other wives, and make ornaments and playthings for
their use. In the friends and servants of her husband

she should confide more than in his other wives.
Also, she must cultivate a fondness for drinking
parties, picnics, fairs and festivals, and for carrying
out all kinds of games and amusements.

In general, a woman who is disliked by her husband and annoyed and distressed by his other wives,
should associate with the favorite wife of her husband as she serves him more than the others. She
should teach this favorite wife all the arts with which
she is acquainted. She should act as the nurse of her
husband's children and having gained over his
friends to her side, should employ them to make him
acquainted with her devotion. In religious ceremonies she should be a leader, and also in vows and
fasts, and should not hold too good an opinion of
herself. When her husband is lying on his bed, she
should go near him only when it is agreeable to him,
and should never rebuke him or show obstinacy in
any way. If her husband happens to quarrel with
any of his other wives, she should reconcile them to
each other, and if he desires to see any woman secretly she should manage to bring about the meeting
between them. She should moreover make herself
acquainted with the weak points of her husband's
character but should always keep them secret, and
on the whole deport herself in such a way as may

lead him to look upon her as a good and devoted wife.

Now a man who marries many wives should act fairly towards them all. He should neither disregard their faults nor reveal to any one wife the love, passion, bodily blemishes, and confidential intimacies of the others. No opportunity should be given to any of them to speak to him of their rivals, and if one of them should begin to speak ill of another, he should chide her severely. The wise husband should praise his wives in different ways. One of them he should please by secret confidences, another by secret respect, and another by secret flattery, and he should please them all by going to gardens, by amusements, by gifts, by honoring their relations, and above all, by loving embraces. A young woman who is of good temper, and who conducts herself according to the precepts of the Holy Writ, wins her husband's attachment and obtains a preference over her many rivals.

The relations of the King with the women in his seraglio are somewhat more complex and formal. The female attendants in the harem should bring flowers, ointments, and clothes from the King's wives to the King. A day or two after he has received them, he should give them as presents to the servants. In the afternoon the King, having dressed and put on his ornaments, should interview the women of the harem, who should also be dressed and decorated with jewels. Then, having given to each of them such respect as may suit the occasion and as they may deserve, he should carry on with them cheerful conversations. Afterwards, he should see such of his wives as may be virgin widows remarried, and after them the concubines and the dancing girls. Of course, each of these should be visited in her own private rooms.

When the King rises from his noonday sleep the woman, whose duty it is to inform him of the wife who is to spend the night with him, should come to him accompanied by the female attendants of that wife. She should also be accompanied by the attendants of other wives who may have been unwell at the time their turns arrived. These attendants should place before the King the ointments and unguents sent by each of these wives, marked with the seal of her ring, and their names and reasons for sending the ointments should be given to the King. After this the King accepts the ointment of one of them, who is then informed that her ointment has been accepted. The wife to whom this happens is considered by her rivals with envious looks—especially if the King happens to be a virile lover, which is seldom the case.

The conduct of a wife in India during menstruation is beset with innumerable restrictions and merits some explanation here. As long as menstruation lasts, she must avoid coitus. Her husband must not approach her sexually under any circumstances nor sleep with her on the same couch. The lawgivers are unanimous in condemning any breach of this rule and raise all sorts of bogies to intimidate forgetful men, such as the loss of vitality, sight, reason, and weakness of offspring.

During her courses, the woman must neither bathe nor decorate herself and must lie on a couch of darba grass, eat nothing but mush and milk, from an earthenware pot, using the flat of her hand or a leaf as a plate. Any violation of this or other special duties will harm her future offspring.

When a woman is in the state of her courses she is isolated and may have no communication with anyone during the three days of her defilement. She must neither bathe nor wash any part of her body nor shed tears. She must be careful not to kill any insect or any living creature. She must not anoint her head with oil nor play games nor use perfumes of any kind. She must not lie on a bed nor sleep during the day. She is forbidden to salute persons of high rank.

On the fourth day, her courses over, she must remove the garments she has been wearing and have them washed immediately. She must then go to the river and purify herself by bathing. After returning to the bank to wash her teeth, she reenters the water and completely immerses herself twenty-four times. After performing other ablutions, she returns home and sends for a Brahman purohita in whose presence she completes her purification by drinking a little consecrated water and some cow's milk. After these ceremonies she is fit to resume her place in society.

XII

The Paradox of Adultery

THE
PARADOX
OF
ADULTERY

It is strangely paradoxical that the Hindus are the most adulterous of peoples and at the same time are governed by the strictest laws against adultery. This paradoxical situation is due to the fact that their profession of faith is diametrically opposed to their

practise. The law-givers are sternly against marital
infidelity and bring the wrath of the heavens down
upon the committers of adultery, whereas the classic
eroticists and venerable sages, as we observed repeatedly, are concerned largely with the art of seducing other men's wives. How reconcile these
contradictory attitudes? Only in India, perhaps, can
black and white be seriously accepted as reverse sides
of the same color. By the most specious and casuistic
reasoning, the eroticists harmonize the condemna-
tion of the law-givers with their own views and thus
salve the skin-deep conscience of the race.

It must be understood that the *Sacred Institutes*
of Manu which are the head and front of all sanctified
morality condemn adultery principally for reasons
of caste. As such behavior tends to blend individuals
of different castes (varna), there can be no higher
crime to Hindu morality or any deeper prejudice.
This caste basis, as we have explained previously,
motivates all aspects of Hindu religion and morality.

According to Manu:

A man formerly accused of adultery with the wives of
others, who secretly converses with another man's wife,
shall pay the first or lowest fine. But a man, not previously
accused, who thus speaks with a woman for some reason-

able cause, shall not incur any guilt, since in him there is no transgression.

He who addresses the wife of another man at a tirtha (a place on the river-bank where women fetch water) outside the village, in a forest, or at the confluence of rivers, shall suffer the punishment for adulterous acts (samgrahana).

Offering gifts to a woman, romping with her, touching her ornaments and dress, sitting with her on a bed—all these are considered adulterous acts.

If a man touches a woman in a lonely spot, with or without her consent, such an act is declared to be adulterous.

A man who is not a Brahman ought to suffer death for adultery; for wives of all the four castes even must always be carefully guarded.

Mendicants, bards, men who have performed the initiatory ceremony of a Vedic sacrifice, and artisans are not prohibited from speaking to married women.

Let no man converse with the wives of others after he has been forbidden to do so; and he who converses with them, in spite of a prohibition, shall be fined one suvarna.

This does not apply to the wives of actors and singers, nor of those who live on the intrigues of their own wives; for such men send their wives to others or, concealing themselves, allow them to hold criminal intercourse.

Yet he who secretly converses with such women, or with female slaves kept by one master, and with female ascetics, shall be compelled to pay a small fine.

The Hindu Art of Love

He who violates an unwilling maiden shall instantly suffer corporal punishment, if his caste be the same as hers.

A maiden who makes advances to a man of high caste, shall not be fined; but she who courts a man of low caste, should be forced to live confined in her house for she is without shame.

A man of low caste who makes love to a maiden of the highest caste shall suffer corporal punishment; he who addresses a maiden of equal caste shall pay the nuptial fee, if her father desires it.

If any man through insolence forcibly contaminates a maiden, two of his fingers shall be instantly cut off, and he shall pay a fine of six hundred panas. A man of equal caste who defiles a willing maiden shall not suffer the amputation of his fingers, but shall pay a fine of two hundred panas in order to deter him from a repetition of the offence.

A damsel who pollutes another damsel must be fined two hundred panas, pay double her nuptial fee, and receive ten lashes with a rod. But a woman who pollutes a damsel shall instantly have her head shaved or two fingers cut off, and be made to ride through the town on a donkey.

If a wife, proud of the greatness of her relatives or her own excellence, violates the duty which she owes to her lord, the King shall cause her to be devoured by dogs in a place frequented by many. The King shall cause the male who commits this offence to be burnt on a red-hot iron bed; they shall put logs under it, until the sinner is burned to death.

A man who is once convicted of adultery, and is again accused within a year, should be fined double; even thus must the fine be doubled for repeated intercourse with a Vratya and a Kandali.

A Sudra who has intercourse with a woman of a twice-born caste, guarded or unguarded, shall be punished in the following manner: if she was unguarded, he loses the offending member and all his property; if she was guarded, he loses everything, even his life.

For intercourse with a guarded Brahmani, a Vaisya shall forfeit all his property after imprisonment for a year; a Kshatriya shall be fined one thousand panas and be shaved with the urine of an ass. If a Vaisya or a Kshatriya has connection with an unguarded Brahmani, the Vaisya should be fined five hundred panas and the Kshatriya one thousand. But even these two, if they offend with a Brahmani, not only guarded but the wife of an eminent man, shall be punished like a Sudra or be burnt in a fire of dry grass.

A Brahman who carnally knows a guarded Brahmani against her will, shall be fined one thousand panas; but he shall be made to pay five hundred if he has connection with a willing one.

Tonsure of the head is ordained for a Brahman instead of capital punishment; but men of other castes shall suffer capital punishment. A Brahman must never be slain though he have committed all possible crimes. He may be banished but his property must not be taken from him nor his body hurt. No greater crime is known on earth than slaying a Brahman; a King, therefore, must not even conceive in his mind the possibility of such a thought.

If a Vaisya approaches a guarded female of the Kshatriya caste, or a Kshatriya a guarded Vaisya woman, they both deserve the same punishment as in the case of an unguarded Brahmani.

A Brahman shall be compelled to pay a fine of one thousand panas if he has intercourse with guarded females of those two castes; for offending with a guarded Sudra female a fine of one thousand panas shall be inflicted on a Kshatriya or a Vaisya.

For intercourse with an unguarded Kshatriya a fine of five hundred panas shall fall on a Vaisya; but for the same offence a Kshatriya shall be shaved with the urine of a donkey or pay the same fine.

A Brahman who approaches unguarded females of the Kshatriya or Vaisya castes, or a Sudra female, shall be fined five hundred panas; but for intercourse with a female of the lowest caste (that is, a Kandali), one thousand.

He who has violated his Guru's bed shall, after confessing his crime, extend himself on a heated iron bed, or embrace the red-hot image of a woman; the mark of a female part should be impressed on his forehead with a hot iron; only by dying can he become pure. Or, having himself cut off his organ and his testicles and having taken them in his joined hands, he must walk straight to

the region of Nirriti (the southwest) until he falls down
dead. Or, carrying the foot of a bedstead, dressed in garments of bark and allowing his beard to grow, he may,
with a concentrated mind, perform during a whole year
the Krikkhra (hard penance), revealed by Pragapati, in
a lonely forest. Or, controlling his organs, he may during three months continuously perform the lunar penance,
subsisting on sacrificial food or barley gruel, in order to
remove the guilt of violating a Guru's bed.

He who has had sexual intercourse with sisters by the
same mother, with the wives of a friend, or of a son, with
unmarried maidens, and with females of the lowest castes,
shall perform the penance prescribed for the violation of
a Guru's bed.

He who has approached the daughter of his father's
sister, who is almost equal to a sister, the daughter of his
mother's sister, or of his mother's full brother, shall perform a lunar penance. A wise man should not take as his
wife any of these three; they must not be wedded because
they are relatives (Sapinda), and he who marries one of
them, sinks low.

A man who has committed a bestial crime, or an unnatural crime with a female, or has had intercourse in
water, or with a menstruating woman, shall perform a
Samtapana Krikkhra. A twice-born man who commits an
unnatural offence with a male, or has intercourse with a
female in a cart drawn by oxen, in water, or in the day-
time, must bathe, dressed in his clothes.

A Brahman who unintentionally approaches a woman

of the Kandala or of any other very low caste, who eats the food of such persons and accepts presents from them, becomes an outcast; but if he does it intentionally, he becomes their equal.

An exceedingly corrupt wife must be confined to one room and compelled to perform the penance which is prescribed for males in cases of adultery. If, being solicited by a man of equal caste, she afterwards is again unfaithful, then a Krikkhra and a lunar penance are prescribed as the means of purifying her.

The sin which a twice-born man commits by dallying one night with a Vrishali, he can remove after three years by subsisting on alms and daily muttering sacred texts.

That King in whose town there lives no adulterer and no committer of assaults, attains the world of Sakra (Indra).

Despite their elaborate classifications on the Art of Love, with its important bypath of adultery, the eroticists agree that there may be seven types of trouble resulting from having intercourse with the wife of another man:

Adultery shortens the period of life
The body becomes spiritless and vigorless
The world derides and reproaches the lover
The lover begins to despise himself
His wealth greatly decreases
He suffers much in this world
And he will suffer more in the world to come.

The Paradox of Adultery

The eroticists attempt another subtle reconciliation of their attitude with the doctrines of Manu by describing how great and powerful monarchs have ruined themselves and their realms by their desire to enjoy the wives of others. For instance, in former days the family of the Ravana, King of Ceylon, was destroyed because he forcibly abducted Sita, the wife of Rama, and this action gave rise to the celebrated Ramayana, one of the most widely translated of Sanscrit epic poems. Vali lost his life for attempting to have connection with Tara, as is fully described in the Kishkinda-kand, a chapter of that history. Kichaka, the Kaurava, together with all his brethren, met with destruction, because he wished to have Draupada, daughter of Drupad, the common wife of the Pandu brothers, as is described in that section of the Mahabharata. These are some of the typical tragedies which have happened to those who coveted other men's wives. The inevitable conclusion is implicit: let none, therefore, attempt adultery.

Of course, declare the eroticists, perpetually justifying the words of Manu to man, there are exceptions. And upon these *exceptions* they build their venerable doctrines. Despite the dire results emanating from the above instances of adultery, it is necessary for a man to have connection with the wife of

another when he becomes a victim of the ten following changes of longing. We have already briefly
alluded to these ten progressive stages of love in the
Theory and Practice of Love in an earlier chapter.
We amplify them here in a somewhat different form
to clarify the subject and refresh the memory of the
reader.

First, when a man is in a state of desire, at a loss to do
anything except to see a particular woman; second, when
he finds his mind wandering, as if he were about to lose
his senses; third, when he is ever losing himself in
thought, wondering how to woo and win the woman in
question; fourth, when he passes restless nights without
the refreshment of sleep; fifth, when his looks become
haggard and his body emaciated; sixth, when he feels
himself growing shameless and departing from all sense
of decency and decorum; seventh, when his riches seem
to take wings and fly away; eighth, when his state of mental intoxication verges upon madness; ninth, when fainting fits come on; and tenth, when he finds himself at
the door of death.

That these states are produced by sexual passion
may be illustrated by an example borrowed from
ancient history. A king named Pururava, a devout
man, once entered upon such a course of mortifica-
tion and austerities that Indra, Lord of the Lower

Heaven, began to fear lest he himself might be dethroned. The god, therefore, in order to interrupt these penances and other religious acts, sent down from Svarga, his own heaven, Urvashi, the most lovely of the nymphs (Apsaras). The king no sooner saw her than he fell in love with her, thinking day and night of nothing but possessing her, till at length he succeeded in his project. Whereupon they both spent a long time in the pleasures of carnal connection. Presently Indra, happening to remember the Apsara, despatched his messenger, one of the heavenly minstrels (Gandharvas), to the world of mortals, and recalled her. Immediately after her departure, the mind of Pururava began to wander; he was no longer able to concentrate his thoughts upon worship and he felt near the verge of death.

When a man has thus allowed himself to be made a slave of desire, he must consult a physician, and the books of medicine which treat upon the subject. If he comes to the conclusion that unless he enjoys his neighbor's wife he will surely die, he should, for the sake of preserving his life, possess her once and once only. If however there is no such irresistible reason, he is by no means justified in enjoying the wife of another person.

The Hindu Art of Love

The sages all counsel that the following special occasions justify a man's committing adultery. There are many other exceptions upon which there is no complete accord and which there is no point in enumerating here because they are really not exceptional cases at all. The ultimate consequence of these "special occasions" is a total nullification of the *Sacred Institutes* of Manu, for the eroticists make the man himself the judge of all these occasions. These are the exceptions upon which there is unanimity of opinion.

When a man thinks thus:

This woman is self-willed and has been previously enjoyed by many others. I may therefore safely resort to her as to a public woman though she belongs to a higher caste than mine, and in so doing I shall not be violating the ordinances of Dharma.

Or: This is a twice-married woman and has been enjoyed by others; there is therefore no objection to my resorting to her.

Or: This woman has gained the heart of her great and powerful husband and exercises a mastery over him, who is a friend of my enemy; if, therefore, she becomes united with me she will cause her husband to abandon my enemy.

Or: This woman will turn the mind of her husband, who is very powerful, in my favor; at present he bears me ill and is intent on doing me some harm.

The Paradox of Adultery

Or: By making this woman my friend I shall gain the object of some friend of mine; or I shall be able to effect the ruin of some enemy; or I shall accomplish some other difficult purpose.

Or: By being united with this woman, I shall kill her husband, and so obtain his vast riches which I covet.

Or: The union of this woman with me is not attended with any danger, and will bring me wealth of which, on account of my poverty and inability to support myself, I am very much in need.

Or: This woman loves me ardently and knows all my weak points; if therefore I am unwilling to be united with her, she will make my faults public and thus tarnish my character and reputation; or she will bring some gross accusation against me, of which it may be hard to clear myself, and I shall be ruined; or she may detach from me her husband who is powerful and yet under control, and will unite him to my enemy, or will herself join the latter.

Or: The husband of this woman has violated the chastity of my wives; I shall therefore return that injury by seducing his wives.

Or: By the help of this woman I shall kill an enemy of the King, who has taken shelter with her, and whom I am ordered by the King to destroy.

Or: The woman whom I love is under the control of this woman; I shall in this way win the woman whom I love beyond all others.

Or: This woman will bring to me a maid, who pos-

sesses wealth and beauty but who is hard to seduce, and
under the control of another.

Or last: My enemy is a friend of this woman's husband; I shall in this way create an enmity between her
husband and him.

The *Kama Sutra* brings the reverse of the medal
to increase the number of justifiable adulteries
which a Hindu may enjoy. The general case is:

Suppose that a woman, having reached the lusty vigor
of her age, happens to become so inflamed with love for
a man, and so aroused by passion that she feels herself
falling into the ten states before described, and likely to
die if her beloved refuses her sexual commerce. Under
these circumstances, the man, after allowing himself to
be importuned for a time, should reflect that his refusal
will cost her life. He should, therefore, enjoy her on one
occasion, but not constantly.

The eroticists, after nullifying the doctrines of
Manu by subtle subterfuge, go even further and
compile lists of wives who are the easiest and most
difficult to seduce. Their list of the former includes:

A wife whose deportment shows signs of immodesty;
a wife fond of conversation; a wife steeped in poverty;
the wife of an imbecile or an impotent person; the wife

of a fat and pot-bellied man; the wife of a cruel man; the wife of a very ugly man; a wife accustomed to stand in the doorway and stare at passersby; wives of changeable disposition; the barren wife, especially if she or her husband desire the blessing of issue; the wife who brags and boasts; the wife who has long been separated from her husband and deprived of her natural refreshment; the wife who has never known the true delight of carnal copulation; and finally, the wife whose mind remains girlish.

On the other hand, wives who can be subdued only with difficulty and upon whom it is not worth while to waste hours of pursuit are as follows:

The happily married wife; the wife whose cold desire and contempt for congress keep her chaste; the wife who is envious of another's prosperity and success; the mother of many children; a dutiful daughter or daughter-in-law; a courteous and respectful wife; an awed wife who fears her parents and her husband; and finally, a wealthy wife, who ever suspects and often wrongly, that the man loves her money better than herself.

XIII

The Role of the Procuress

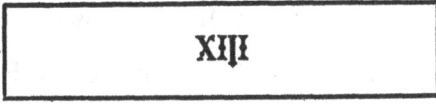

THE
ROLE
OF
THE
PROCURESS

It is natural that in India where sexual love is sanctified to a higher degree than in any other race in the world, that the role of the procuress should be not only an important one but also complex with innumerable colors. It is extremely difficult for an

The Hindu Art of Love

American to understand the role of the Hindu procuress as it is conditioned primarily by child marriages. When a man looks at a woman in India and is attracted to her, he at once thinks of seduction. Such relations as platonic friendships and mutual interests of one sort or another between the sexes apart from seduction are incomprehensible to the Hindu. When there are no other means of bringing together a man and a woman, the services of a procuress are sought. Unlike our notions, there is no stigma attached to the profession of a procuress in India. On the contrary, she is regarded there as a friend of the family and is a natural and important social type.

Addalaka says that when a man and woman are not personally acquainted with each other, and have not shown each other any signs of desire, the employment of a procuress is useless. The followers of Babhravya, on the other hand, affirm that even though they are personally unacquainted, but have shown each other casual signs of interest there is a sufficient reason to employ a procuress. Gonikaputra asserts that a procuress should be employed, provided the man and woman are acquainted with each other, even though no gestures of interest have passed between them. Vatsya Yana however maintains that even though they are not personally acquainted and have not shown each other any signs of interest, they are both likely to place confidence in a procuress, and win to the accomplishment of their mutual desire.

The women who best serve as procuresses are: a gardener's wife; a woman who is a personal friend; a widow; a nurse; a dancing girl; a woman engaged in manual or mechanical arts; a servant or maid to the women of the family; an attendant as distinguished from a slave girl; a neighbor who goes from house to house speaking sweet words; a woman with whom love and enjoyment can be freely discussed; a young woman under sixteen; a female ascetic or religious mendicant; a woman who sells milk and buttermilk; and a woman who can be called "Mistress Grandmother."

Procuresses should possess the following qualities: skillfulness; boldness; absence of confusion; freedom from shyness; knowledge of the hidden meaning behind speech and actions; good manners; tact; ingenuity in business; speed of comprehension; resourcefulness; and flexibilty of temperament.

The procuress should wheedle herself into the confidence of the woman by acting according to the latter's disposition. She should try to make her hate or despise her husband by holding artful conversations with her, by telling her about medicines for procuring children, by comparing her with other people, by tales about the wives of other men, and by praising her beauty, wisdom, generosity, and good nature. The purport of all the conversation of the procuress should center about this attitude: "It is a pity that you, who are so excellent a woman in every way, should be possessed of a husband of this kind. Beautiful lady, he is not even fit to serve you."

The procuress should also talk to the woman about the weakness of the passion of her husband, his jealousy, his roguery, his ingratitude, his aversion to enjoyments, his dullness, his manners, and all his other faults with which she may be acquainted. She should particularly stress that failing in him by which the wife is most affected. If the wife is a deer-woman and the husband a hare-man, his faults of character rather than temperament should be remarked. If he is a hare-man and she a mare-woman, his weakness of passion should be emphasized above all other faults.

The procuress should describe in glowing colors the intense love of the man whose suit she is handling, and as the other's confidence and affection increase, she should revolve her purpose about the following theme: "Hear this, O Beautiful Lady, that this man, born of a good family, having seen you, has gone mad on your account. The poor young man, who is tender of nature, has never been distressed in such a way before, and it is highly probable that he will succumb under his present affliction, and experience the pains of death."

If the woman listens with a favorable ear, and shows some signs of pleasure, the procuress should return to this theme on her following visits. She should also embellish her conversation with stories of Ahalya, the wife of the sage Gautama, seduced by Indra, the King of the Gods, of Shakuntala and Dushyanti, and others suitable as may be for the occasion. These stories should be interpolated with remarks on the strength of the man who adores her passionately, his skill in the sixty-four arts of enjoyment, his good looks, and his liaisons with praiseworthy women, no matter whether this last condition be true or not.

After a number of visits, the procuress should carefully note the behavior of the woman. If the man be favorable disposed, the following changes will take place in her: She will address the procuress with a smile, seat herself close beside her, and ask,

"Where have you been? What have you been doing? Where have you dined? Where have you slept? Where have you been sitting?"

The procuress should give the woman presents, such as betel nuts and betel leaves, perfumes, flowers, and rings which the man has asked the procuress to deliver to the woman as a token of his love. On these gifts should be impressed the marks of the man's teeth and nails denoting passion and the desire for congress. If he sends cloth as a gift, he should weave with saffron an image of his hands joined together as if in earnest entreaty. The procuress should also show to the woman ornamental figures of all sorts cut in leaves, together with ear ornaments, and chaplets made of flowers containing love letters expressive of the desire of the man. The procuress should attempt to induce the woman to send affectionate presents to the man in return. After they have exchanged gifts, a meeting may be arranged between them on the confidence of the procuress.

Moreover, the woman will soon find occasion to meet the procuress in lonely places and converse with her there, will muse contemplatively, draw long sighs, give her presents, remember her on festivities, depart from her with a wish to see her again, and say to her jestingly, "Oh, well-speaking woman, why do you speak of such disloyal matters to me?" Nevertheless, the woman will discourse with the procuress on the sin of her congress with the man, will not tell her of any previous visits or conversations which she may already have had with him, but wish to be asked about these. As soon as the woman laughs at stories of the man's desire, without reproaching him in any way, the battle is practically won.

When the woman manifests her love in the manner above described, the procuress should increase it by bringing to her love-tokens from the man. But if the woman is not yet acquainted with the man personally, the procuress should at once arrange such a visit.

The disciples of Babhravya assert that this meeting should take place only upon the following occasions: when going to a temple of a Deity; when attending fairs, garden parties, theatrical performances, marriages, sacrifices, festivals and funerals; when going to the river to bathe; and also at times of natural calamities, pillages of brigands, or hostile invasions of the country. Gonikaputra is of the opinion, however, that these meetings should be limited to the abodes of female friends, mendicants, astrologers, and ascetics. But practical Vatsya Yana opines that only such places are suitable which have proper means of ingress and egress, and where arrangements have been made to prevent accidental interruption, and when a man has once entered the house, he can also leave it at the proper time without any disagreeable encounter.

Although the eroticists differ more widely upon the duties of the procuress than upon almost any other phase of love and seduction, they generally agree upon eight distinct types of such women. These are:

A procuress who assumes the whole burden of the matter

A procuress who conducts only a part of the affair

A procuress who is the bearer of a letter only

A procuress who acts on her own account

The procuress of an innocent young woman

A wife who serves as a procuress

A mute procuress

A procuress who acts the part of the wind

A woman who, having served the mutual passion of a man and a woman, brings them together through her own methods exclusively is called a procuress who takes upon herself the whole burden of the matter. This type is chiefly employed when the man and woman are already acquainted with each other, and have conversed together. In such cases he may be sent by the man (as is done in all other cases) or by the woman. The above appellation is also given to a procuress who, perceiving that a man and woman are suited to each other, tries to bring about a union between them even if they are not known to each other.

A procuress who, perceiving that some part of the affair has already been arranged, or that the advances on the part of the man are already made, conducts the rest of the matter is called a procuress who performs only a limited part of the liaison.

A procuress who simply carries messages between a man and woman who love each other but who are unable to meet frequently, is called the bearer of a letter or message. This name is also given to one who is sent by either of the lovers to inform the other of the time and place of the next meeting.

A woman who herself goes to a man and tells him of her having enjoyed sexual union with him in a dream, and who gives him a token bearing the marks of her teeth and nails, and who informs him that she is aware that she was formerly desired by him, and who asks him privately whether she or his wife is the better looking, such a person is called a procuress who acts on her own account. The appellation is also given to a woman who, having made an agreement with some other woman to act as her procuress, tempts the man to herself and disregards the other woman's plans. This appellation also applies to a man who, acting as a procurer for another and having no previous connection with the woman in question, seduces her himself, thus preventing her seduction by the other man.

A woman who has gained the confidence of an innocent young wife, and has discovered that the young wife's husband is indifferent to her, and if this woman teaches her the art of recovering his love and exciting him for enjoyment, such a woman is called the procuress of an innocent young woman.

When a man compels his wife to gain the confidence of a woman whom he wants to enjoy, and has his wife eulogize to her his wisdom and virility, such a woman is called a wife who serves as a procuress. In this case, the feelings of the woman towards the husband should also be made known through the wife.

When under some pretext, a man sends a girl or female servant to a woman whom he desires, and places a letter in the bouquet of flowers or in the parcel containing the gift of ear ornaments, or if he marks something about her with his teeth or nails, the girl or female servant is called a mute procuress.

A woman who carries a message to a woman which has a double meaning or which relates to some past transaction, or which is unintelligible to other people, is called a procuress who acts the part of the wind.

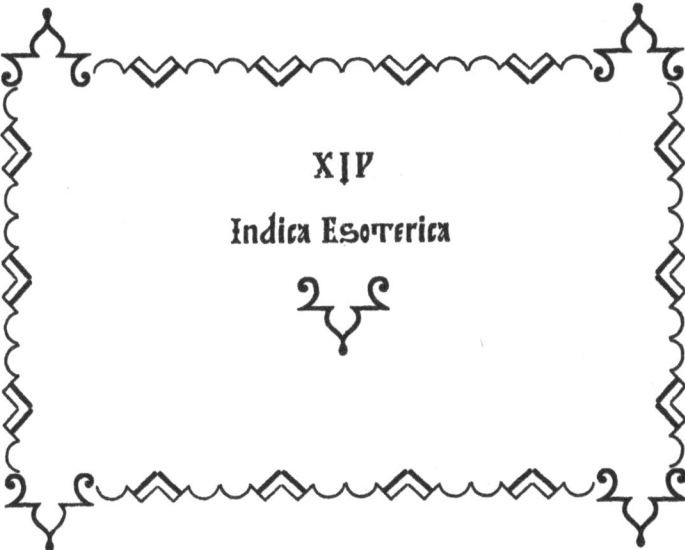

XII

Indica Esoterica

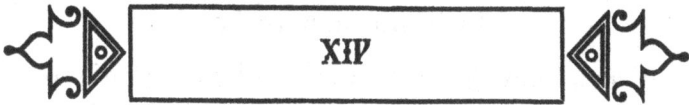

INDICA

ESOTERICA

By this time, the serious reader must be thoroughly aware of the fact that the Hindu Art of Love is fundamentally and intricately interwoven with two religious concepts of existence: first, child marriage, and second, the caste system. It is for this rea-

257

son, as we have seen, that all the Hindu erotic treatises deal with sexuality in a spirit of utmost gravity and in the minutest details discuss the byplays of love as if they were temple rituals. No wonder that in no other country in the world do men devote themselves so exclusively with the minutest sexual characteristics of women.

It is really impossible to enter any phase of Hindu love without referring again and again to their child marriages. Without this system the entire glorification of the ganika could not be possible, and as we have already noted, it is the ganika and her place in Hindu society more than anything else which lends color to Hindu passion. Incredible as it may seem, the Hindus regard it as one of the greatest religious disgraces if parents do not marry their daughters before the first appearance of menstruation, which occurs there usually at the age of ten or eleven. Many of the eroticists assert that should a girl begin to menstruate before she leaves her father's house in marriage, the father must be punished as if he had destroyed a foetus. In such cases the daughter also loses caste. It is for this reason that child marriages have perdured in India since the memory of man and been sanctified by the weight of uncounted centuries. This pre-puberty concept of marriage is held in even greater regard than maternity among us.

It is this custom of child marriage which explains so many of the childish aspects of courtship and post-marital relationships which we have discussed in previous chapters. This custom also serves to explain the glorification of the ganika and the importance of the procuress, both of which play such prominent parts in Hindu passion and seduction.

As for the endogamous caste system which prevents inter-class marriage or sexual intimacy, with frequent exceptions already pointed out in this volume, it is impossible to discuss this supreme structure of Hindu society without losing oneself in the endless ramifications of rank and class. A few brief general remarks are all which we may allow ourselves to set down here. The Hindu castes rank according to the number of transmigrations which the soul is supposed to have undergone, and its consequent proximity to, or distance from, re-absorption into the divine essence, or intellectual abyss whence it has sprung. Hardly in any other race, ancient or modern, has tyranny placed one class of human beings so far above another, as the sacred Brahmans, whose souls are approaching a reunion with their divine source, transcend the wretched outcasts who are without any rank in the hierarchy. These "untouchables" are supposed to have all the long, humiliating, and painful transmigrations yet before them. Should the most respectable and opulent of these degraded mortals happen to touch the poorest and most worthless person of the highest caste, the offence is punishable with death in many Hindu districts. Even to be within reach of his shadow, is to be defiled. As all the castes are hereditary, the soul being supposed to descend into the lower castes for punishment and to ascend into the others for reward, the degradation with all its evils is without hope even in posterity. Loss of caste is therefore the most dreadful punishment that a Hindu can suffer, as it affects both his body and soul, extends beyond the grave, and may reduce him and his posterity forever to a condition below that of an animal.

This caste system naturally leads to stagnation in almost all aspects of social and economic life. It also presupposes the simplicity and naïve acceptance of things which is so characteristic of the Hindu and which shocks an American or Englishman during his first months in India. At the same time this simplicity inevitably leads to hypocritical and moralistic paradoxes of sexuality which are only too common throughout India.

The Hindus blandly accept with atavistic sensuality the mutual appeal of men and women for two purposes: pleasure and progeny. They do not construct moral codes of sexual honor and chastity but simply, fulfilling their instincts of pleasure and progeny, revolve their behavior about these feelings to the point of ritualistic satiety. They read their classic treatises on Kama, pleasure, and guide their conduct according to its hedonistic doctrines.

It is curious to watch the embarrassment of Americans in India when they find themselves ogled on the streets by inviting feminine eyes which boldly seem to be estimating the fingers'-length of their linga and virility. It never seems to enter the heads of these Hindu girls that such behavior can be offensively obscene, and this free attitude pervades the works of their most venerable sages.

From this same attitude arises their love for classification which requires sensuous and simple minds. We have seen the detailed analyses of nayaka and nayika, in previous chapters. The same influence informs all their intellectual products. It is apparent again in their rich sexual symbolism. The man indicates his desire for a woman by certain private signs. The woman knows very well what his intentions are and has at her disposal a number of symbols to indicate her coyness, fear, shame, distrust, lack of opportunity, and compliance.

The mediatory system of a procuress is based on the same ends: a gradual mutual understanding as to means and purposes. The breaking down of a woman's resistance, while really just so much camouflage, is the best of sauces to increase the man's appetite. If he is fit and pleasing, the woman is willing. If she pretends reluctance, the man understands that she needs more coaxing and that it is his task to find the right opportunity to bring about her submission.

The entire Art of Seduction is based on this principle: No woman's fortress is impregnable. It is the duty of the man to understand and make use of his opportunities. He must place himself in a position where he can choose the right time, the right place and the right mood. This is the kernel of the teachings of the eroticists who bend every effort to educate the man on the subject of woman: her moods and dispositions, her nature and temperament, how to recognize her periods of intensest longing, when she can be made so, and the quickest means of making her amorous in general, and towards him in particular.

The main point is to draw the attention of the

woman to the man himself. She must be made to recognize him as a person of some influence, learning or talent, in short, some quality that will make him stand out from other men, and cause her thoughts to be on him. Naturally, if the man cannot gain her attention, there can be no union. But once he has caused her to single him out, half the battle is won. A man can dispense with all the qualities of wealth, high learning and good birth, but he should master one special field upon which she can rivet her attentions and sympathies.

As this volume has indicated throughout, the eroticists are never at a loss for suggestions to bring about the woman's pleasure in congress. We have not hitherto alluded to the *apadravyas*, the appliances fixed in and around the lingam, whether permanently or temporarily during coitus, to heighten her excitement. Although there are an endless variety of these appliances throughout India, it is not our purpose here to describe them or their methods of employment.

In southern India, the lingam is transversely pierced with a sharp instrument and the aperture gradually increased by inserting every few weeks a larger piece of reed than the piece which is withdrawn. When the aperture is sufficiently large, the man inserts in it apadravyas of various shapes, such as the round, the round on one side, the wooden mortar, the flower, the armlet, the bone of the heron, the collection of eight balls, the lock of hair, the place where four roads meet, and other appliances named according to their shapes and uses. The outside surfaces of all these apradavyas are rough and irregular in order to increase the enjoyment of the woman in congress. The eroticists are also quick to suggest various ways of enlarging the lingam. One method is to rub it alternately with the bristles of certain insects and special oils, each treatment to last for ten nights. After a while, the lingam will swell considerably. The man must then lie on a cot and allow the swollen member to hang down through a hole in the cot. Afterwards he assuages the pain induced by the swelling by the application of cool concoctions. This method of enlargement is called suka and is very widespread because the swelling usually lasts during the lifetime of the individual.

There are quite a number of other practises which serve the same purpose, most of them requiring frictional treatment with certain indigenous plants. Some of these practises are supposed to induce swellings lasting only a few days whereas other treatments lead to more lasting results.

Indica Esoterica

The classic eroticists compile extensive lists of
herbs and plants which have aphrodisiacal qualities.
As most of the plants are indigenous only to India
and are altogether unknown to us, we give them no
space here. Most of these recipes are for anointing
the lingam but Vatsya Yana and others include
charms bordering on magic for the purpose of attracting and satisfying women. Kalyana Malla's list
of one hundred and thirty prescriptions is a veritable
pharmacœpium of sexual medicines, cosmetics, unguents, charms, and nostrums. Some of the most
curious and important ones are employed for the
following purposes:

For hastening the paroxysm of woman
For delaying the climax in man
For increasing a man's virility tenfold
For thickening and elongating the lingam
For narrowing and contracting the yoni
For destroying the body hair
For ensuring easy labor in childbirth
For limiting the number of children
For raising and hardening pendulous breasts

Perhaps no better explanation for the preoccupation of the Hindus with sexual knowledge can be
found than in the words of the *Ananga Ranga:*

265

The Hindu Art of Love

"The great princely sage and archpoet, Kalyana Malla, versed in all the arts, after consulting many wise and holy men, and having examined the opinions of many poets, and extracted the essence of their wisdom, composed, with a view of pleasing his sovereign, a work which was called *Ananga Ranga*.

"May it ever be appreciated by the discerning, for it hath been dedicated to those who are desirous of studying the art and mystery of man's highest enjoyment, and to those who are best acquainted with the science and practice of dalliance and love-delight.

"It is true that no joy in the world of mortals can compare with that derived from the knowledge of the Creator. Second, however, and subordinate only to this, are the satisfaction and pleasure arising from the possession of a beautiful woman. Men, it is true, marry for the sake of undisturbed congress, as well as for love and comfort, and often they obtain handsome and attractive wives. But they do not give them plenary contentment, nor do they themselves thoroughly enjoy their charms. The reason of which is, that they are purely ignorant of the Scripture of Love, the Kama Shastra; and, despising the difference between the several kinds of women, they regard them only from an animal point of view. Such men must be looked upon as foolish and unintelligent; and this book is composed with the object of preventing lives and loves from being wasted in similar manner, and the benefits to be derived from its study are set forth:

"It is good to know that if husband and wife live together in close agreement, as one soul in a single body, they shall be happy in this world and in that to come. Their good and charitable actions will be an example to mankind, and their peace and harmony will effect their salvation. No one yet has written a book to prevent the separation of the married pair and to show them how they may pass through life in union. Seeing this, I composed the treatise, offering it to the God Pandurang.

"And thus all you who read of the Art of Love shall know how delicious an instrument is woman, when artfully played upon; how capable she is of producing the most exquisite harmony; of executing the most complicated variations and of giving the divinest pleasures.

"Let me therefore conclude with the benefits to be derived from the study of the Art of Love: The man who knoweth the Art of Love and who understandeth the thorough and varied enjoyment of woman, as advancing age cooleth his passions, learneth to think of his Creator, to study religious subjects, and to acquire divine knowledge. Hence he is freed from further transmigration of souls, and when the tale of his days is duly told, he goeth direct with his wife to heaven (svarga)."

According to the author, "every stanza of the *Ananga Ranga* carries a double meaning and may be interpreted in two ways, either mystical or amatory." This commingling of mysticism with sexual pleasure informs the entire spirit of Hindu eroticism and is intimately related with the worship of the lingam. This religious symbol originated in the dim backward and abysm of time, thousands of years before recorded history, and is still practised in India today. Nor has religious reverence for the yoni been lacking. A symbol combining both the lingam and the yoni is held to be the divine symbol of Shiva, the Reproducer, the third member of the Hindu creative trinity, and is to be found in almost all the temples of India. It is usually placed in the inmost sanctuary, sculptured in granite, marble or ivory, often crowned with flowers, and surmounted by a golden star. Lamps are kept burning before it, and on festive occasions it is illuminated by a lamp with seven branches, supposed to represent the planets.

These linga are made of granite, marble, ivory and precious wood, and are generally of very large proportions, some reaching the enormous size of two hundred feet and measuring fifty feet in circumference. The temples of the lingam are to be seen in great numbers on the banks of the Ganges, especially in the neighborhood of Calcutta. Their presence near the river invests them with greater sanctity than if built in the interior of the country. Adjoining each of these temples is a small house, open in front, for the accommodation of the devotees who come there to die in sight of the river. The temples are built in groups of eight or ten, although at some places as many as a hundred are located within short range of one another.

The priests belonging to these temples are sworn to the strictest chastity, and, as they are nude while officiating, any carnal excitations of the imagination would be manifest in their external organs. Such sacrilege is punishable by the summary stoning to death of the uncontrollable priest.

While the linga in the temples are of gigantic proportions, those used for domestic worship are but a few inches in height. The latter are worn as amulets or charms about the neck by Hindus when engaged in prayer.

This worship of the lingam is an important and necessary religious rite, and, when properly performed in accordance with the prescribed ritual, is a most elaborate ceremony, consisting of sixteen essential requisites, including a prefatory bath of purification by the worshipper, the bathing of the lingam with clear butter, honey and the juice of sugar cane, the offering of flowers, incense, lamps, fruits and various kinds of prepared edibles, the repetition of prayers, and the walking about and bowing before the image.

The Hindu Art of Love

Worship may be performed either in a temple or in a purified place, but is considered most efficacious when performed on the bank of a holy river before a lingam formed of clay. Hindus of every caste and of both sexes mould images of this symbol with the clay of the Ganges every morning after bathing, and worship before them, bowing, presenting offerings, and repeating incantations. Upon the completion of the ceremony the lingam is thrown into the river.

Postscript

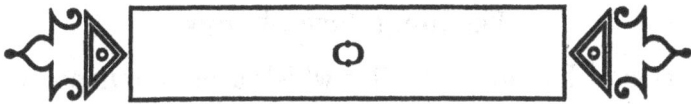

POSTSCRIPT

The serious adult reader for whom this work has been compiled will no doubt be intrigued by a few problems now that he has finished this volume. In self-defense the author must repeat that the ambiguous attitude towards sexual candor in English-speaking countries has tended to obscure certain aspects of Hindu sensuality which a more outspoken treatment would have obviated. This cannot be avoided as long as self-appointed censors and reformers confuse pornography with serious erotica and do their misguided utmost to suppress the latter while they blink at the former.

The reader will find it difficult to appreciate how the Hindus, who are one of the purest of races by the criterion of sexual perversion, can be one of the most impure of races by the criterion of sexual unrestraint. For the curious fact is that hardly any country in the world can boast of so little sodomy, lesbianism, homosexuality, bestiality, and other perversions as India. The ordinary Hindu knows next to nothing of any form of carnal cohabitation other than the normal relations between man and woman. The explanation of this anomaly lies in the Hindu's inordinate absorption in the complicated intricacies of normal congress. The extent of homosexuality and lesbianism in Europe would astonish the Hindu no less than his supersubtle refinements of passion would astonish the European.

Another problem which arises is this: Why is religion, which is diametrically opposed to sensuality in western civilization, so intimately allied to sensuality among the Hindus? This antithesis is the key and crux of Indic morality with its obscure and manifold interweavings with lingam worship.

We have tried, in the course of this volume, to make convincingly clear the fact that the three fundamental tap-roots of Hindu civilization are the caste system, the child-marriage system, and their peculiar Art of Love. Disregarding the first two as alien to our purpose, we cannot evade the conviction that there is something essentially immoral with the Hindu preoccupation with sex. There is a rooted instinct in the Christian which is truer than any scientific reason, a faith which lies deeper than a thousand reasons, and it is this instinct which turns us away from the sexual bent of mind which characterizes the Hindu. Perhaps the noblest lesson which the Hindu can teach us is that we are not as constitutionally amorous as he is, and this explains our lack of a complicated art of love. It is this omission in us which impels us to strive towards spiritual matters, strivings towards faith, hope, and charity, which make no appeal to the Hindu.

One final word. The judgment by results, the ultimate estimate of time from which there is no escape, bears out our remarks. The stagnation of Hindu civilization is due as much to their sensuousness as to their caste system and child-marriages. With the

The Hindu Art of Love

rarest of exceptions, the Hindus have contributed no profound ideas to the modern world, no extraordinary discoveries, no unforgetable acts of courage, no world-famous teachers. Yet India possesses infinite advantages of climate, population, natural resources, and extent of territory. Verily, the Hindu Art of Love moves against the invisible moral laws of this world and the ripening spirit which subserves them.

The End